Nourish your Gut

Over 100 grain, gluten, starch, dairy, yeast, and sugar-free recipes for the entire family to enjoy

Daniela Man

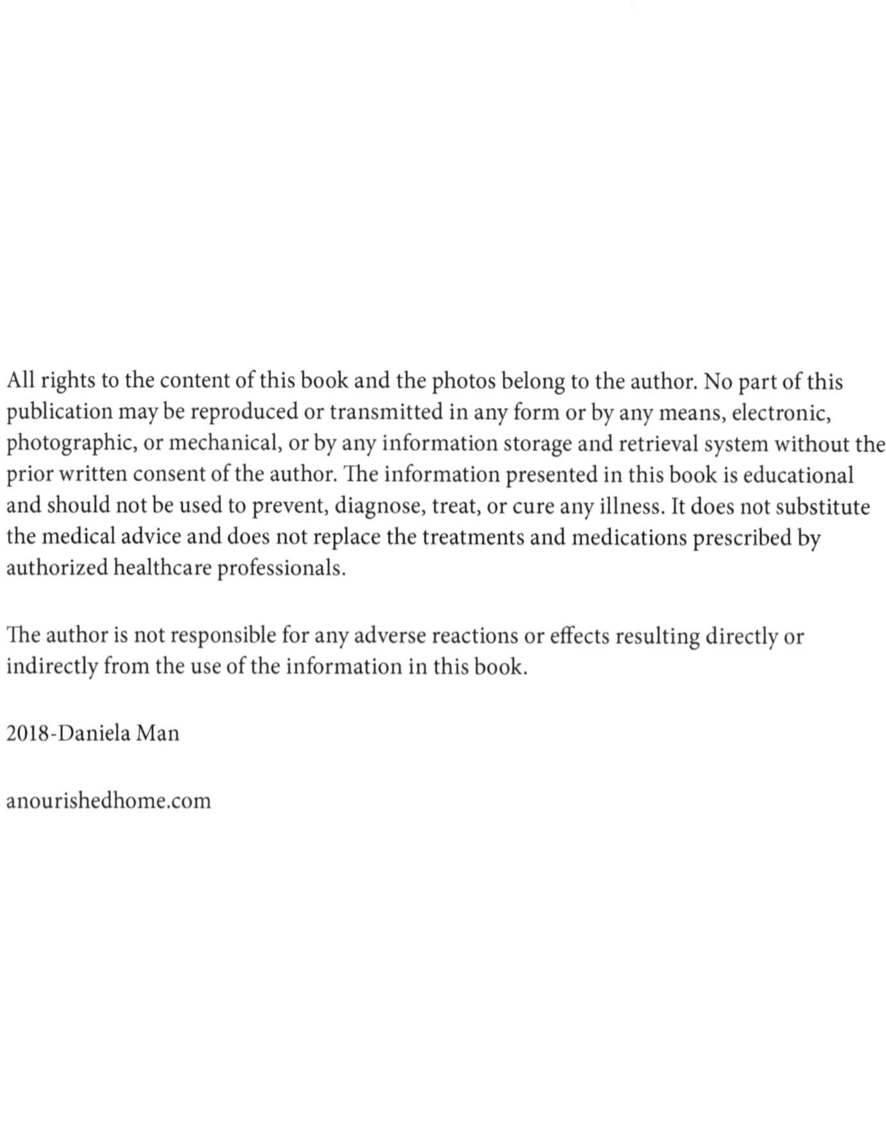

To my children, Andrei and Alexandru and to all of you who are on the path to true health!

May these recipes bring you joy and beautiful memories with your loved ones!

Contents

Breakfast

Lunch & Dinner

Breads

Desserts

Daniela Man is a book author, blogger, a therapist for alternative and complementary therapies, nutrition, diet, life coach and nutritionist specialized in the Specific Carbohydrate Diet Dairy-Free.

After diagnosing her child with autism, Daniela has devoted herself to studying alternative methods of treatment and has managed to help her own child overcome his serious health condition and regain his speech by implementing this specific diet and various complementary therapies. Besides the extraordinary results with her own child, Daniela has brought great results to the lives of many people, results that you can read about on her personal blog, www.anourishedhome.com, and today she offers support to families from all over the world.

She published the book named "Introduction to the Specific Carbohydrate Diet Dairy-Free" that contains scientific explanations, practical applications and recipes specifically created for children diagnosed with autism as well as for those suffering from various autoimmune diseases and major gut problems, that is a beacon of light for many people in their struggle for a decent life.

Because she did not want her family to feel limited by introducing this diet, Daniela has come to create delicious recipes, rich in nutrients and so like ordinary dishes, that you cannot even tell a difference.

This book brings a lot of value to everyone who suffers from chronic inflammation, autoimmune diseases, autism or ADHD, chronic fatigue, depression, serious intestinal illness, dementia, Alzheimer's, allergies, or food intolerances, but it can be a lifestyle for everyone who wants to reduce complex sugars from their diet.

Since chronic inflammation is on the rise and the common point of triggering many diseases, a grain-free, dairy, sugar or even starch-free diet helps the body and can reverse an inflammatory process. Most people come back to regain their full health following the implementation of this diet.

Daniela is currently partnering with doctors, scientists, and specialists from all over the world and has also started a nonprofit organization in Romania through which she wants to gather the necessary levers for families who need support in their struggle with the effects of autistic spectrum disorders. By purchasing this book, you are supporting her work and her mission to heal the world.

We wish it helps you and brings you joy as well, along with your dear ones!

Note from the author

Usually, festive occasions are a great opportunity to gather with all our family and friends, with our loved ones, to create beautiful experiences and priceless memories.

But when some of us have certain dietary prohibitions or suffer from chronic diseases, these festive occasions can bring frustration, the feeling of separation, or even the pain that we cannot consume the foods we were so accustomed to and that have brought us so much joy!

I have created all these recipes for you all, and I promise you that they are just as delicious as, or even more special than the dishes you've got used to so far!

This book contains only recipes without grains, without starches, sugar, dairy, or yeast. Various grain flours are replaced by nuts and seeds. Dairy milk is replaced with nut, seeds or coconut milk, and sugar is replaced with honey, the only natural sweetener that can be digested regardless of the health state of the small intestine or the degree of inflammation of the body.

Further down I introduce you to the main ingredients in these recipes and the most used utensils in my kitchen.

You can find a complete list and more details about the permitted or forbidden foods in the Specific Carbohydrate Diet Dairy-Free, on my blog, www.anourishedhome. com or in my first book, "Introduction to the Specific Carbohydrate Diet Dairy-Free in Treating Autism and ADHD Symptoms, Celiac disease, Crohn's disease, ulcerative colitis and irritable bowel syndrome."

I wish you only beautiful memories and I would love to hear your story on my blog, or on any other "A Nourished Home" social media channels.

Sending you, my love!

The most-often used products in my pantry

Almond flour

It is obtained from the finest grinding of the raw almonds and is rich in antioxidants, minerals, vitamins, and fatty acids, and is an excellent substitute for grain flour.

Try to buy fine, skin-free flour, to obtain the best and healthier dough.

Coconut flour

It is a fiber-rich flour made from finely milled coconut pulp after drying. It is also a wonderful alternative for those who have walnut allergies or gluten intolerance, but it absorbs a lot of fluid, so I usually use it in combination with other types of flour or coconut oil.

It has an affordable price, and it is advisable to buy the organic type.

Occasionally, I use combinations of other types of flours made from walnuts and seeds, such as macadamia nuts, pumpkin seeds, or hazelnuts, but mostly I use almond flour and coconut flour.

Coconut oil

It is rich in saturated fat and fatty acids, with incredible health properties and its composition remains unchanged even at high temperatures, making it ideal for baking or roasting.

It is used both in the preparation of dishes as well as for beauty products and is indispensable from our home. Try to buy organic, cold pressed coconut oil, without the chemical additives used in this process.

Olive oil

This cold-pressed oil is rich in monounsaturated fatty acids, antioxidants, vitamins, and enzymes and has great health benefits. We always use it raw, in salads or in skin care products.

Hemp oil

It is obtained by cold pressing hemp seeds, and it is one of the healthiest natural oils with an ideal ratio of 3:1 between omega 6 and omega 3essential fatty acids, so important for the healthy development of the brain and cognitive functions.

It is consumed in salads or hot meals, directly on the plate, do not heat it much.

Ghee

Ghee is obtained by boiling butter, and it originates in India, where it is used daily even nowadays. The clarified butter is rich in omega 3 and essential amino acids, in vitamins A, D and E, helps reducing inflammation and digestion and has a high flash point of 250 degrees Celsius - so I often use it in different recipes cooked in the oven or for sautéing. Boiling removes casein and significantly reduces the amount of lactose in the butter, therefore those with intolerance to casein or lactose can consume ghee.

Honey

Honey is the only natural sweetener approved by the Specific Carbohydrate Diet and, as such, the only sweetener that we can use in both cold and hot dishes. Even if enzymes are destroyed by heat, honey retains many of its properties and the most important thing is that it can be digested even if the intestine is only partially functional. Just be careful to buy real, good quality honey, not modified by the addition of sugar or other ingredients.

Milk

It is allowed and advisable to use vegetable milk obtained from nuts and seeds, such as almond milk, cashew milk, hemp milk or sesame milk. The favorite in our home is cashew milk.

Coconut cream

It is denser and thicker than coconut milk and is found either separately in stores or it remains on the surface of coconut milk and can be skimmed with a tablespoon. It is used as a cream, in sauces and in sweet foods, in the composition of dough or for frosting.

Coconut butter

Unlike coconut oil, coconut butter is made from the entire coconut core and is a whole product. It is much harder than coconut oil and is very useful for frosting and raw vegan products because it preserves the creams without cooking, as it hardens when refrigerated. Just like coconut oil, it has many health benefits and is indicated to be organic, obtained exclusively by cold processing, without additives or chemicals.

Spices

All spices used in our kitchen are purchased individually, from organic sources or certified sources, and are gluten, sugar, additives or preservatives-free.

Look out for the ingredients and check the packaging to not be processed in units that pack or manipulate cereals, dairy, sugar, or other grains to avoid contamination.

Himalayan salt

Himalayan salt crystals contain 84 minerals that are found in the human body and are naturally rich in iodine, in an easy to assimilate form. It is currently considered the purest form of salt available and has pink to dark red shades due to the rich minerals and iron content. Its regular consumption provides the body with essential minerals, trace elements and electrolytes.

Natural sea salt, without the addition of iodine

Sea salt in its pure and unaltered form contains 82 minerals that it takes from seawater, extremely beneficial and important for the health of the human body. If you buy it in its natural form, avoid excess iodine and at the same time anti-agglomerants used to prevent salt from sticking together to moisture.

Utensils used in my kitchen

Measuring utensils

The most important thing for me was to be efficient in the kitchen and to use my time as productively as possible. I'm not very keen on using the scale, and therefore I prefer the type of measuring devices from the American cuisine, that is, in cups and in tablespoons, not in grams.

All my recipes in this book are based on these units of measure.

You can buy these utensils from many online stores. They have different capacities: 1 cup is equivalent to 250 ml, 1/2 cup 125 ml, 1/3 cup is equivalent to 80 ml and 1/4 cup is equivalent to 60 ml.

1 tablespoon is equivalent to 15 ml, ½ tablespoon is equivalent to 7,5 ml, 1 teaspoon is equivalent to 5 ml, ½ teaspoon is equivalent to 2 ml and ¼ teaspoon is equivalent to 1 ml.

Food processor

I think it's the most-often used device in my kitchen. I was lucky enough to be gifted a performance food processor from my sister and I have been using it constantly from the very day I received it. I came up with many recipes using this food processor to mix everything faster and save time and energy. Besides the doughs that are incredibly easy to make in this food processor, I can chop, cut, and even make shakes with it. I recommend you invest in such a device because it makes your kitchen activity so much easier.

Vegetable spiralizer

This is an utensil that allows a lot of creativity and helps you get pasta from vegetables easily and quickly. All you need is your favorite sauce and dinner is ready.

I find it extremely useful in fresh salad combinations as well.

I only use pots that are certified to contain no harmful materials, such as aluminum or Teflon.

I prefer cooking pots made of stainless steel or materials such as ceramics, glass, or porcelain.

The baking molds I use are either made of silicone, glass or ceramic. Baking trays for bread or pies with grain-free dough are usually smaller because the ingredients used are much richer in nutrients and are consumed in smaller quantities and, at the same time, they are more expensive. Usually, my loaf pan is 20 cm long and 7 cm wide (8x3 inches), and the pie pan has a diameter of 20 cm (8 inches).

Breakfast

Rolled vegetable omlette

Ingredients

- 1 white onion, chopped
- ½ cup of thin cut bacon
- 1 cup of chopped Oyster mushrooms
- ½ cup of fresh peas
- 6 eggs
- 1 spoon of fresh green parsley, chopped
- salt, pepper and paprika to taste
- 1 spoon of dried inactive yeast (omit during the first 6 months of diet)
- 1 spoon of ghee

Preparation

Heat a frying pan over the fire and bake the bacon until it shrinks and becomes crispy. Add the onion and cook until it changes color and becomes translucid. Then add the mushrooms, the peas, and the condiments.

Sauté in the pan with the lid on, at low heat. If need be, add a spoon or two of plain water to make sure the peas are cooked properly. At the end add the dried yeast and mix well.

Beat the 6 eggs in a bowl with a little sea salt.

Remove the cooked vegetables from the pan and leave them aside, on a plate or else prepare another frying pan to cook the eggs.

Cook the eggs on low heat and carefully turn the omlette on the other side. When it is ready, set it on a plate, add the vegetables on top and roll slowly.

Cut and serve warm.

Mini mushroom bun chicken burger with avocado

Ingredients

- 3 large mushrooms, stems removed (champignon or boletus)
- half a chicken breast
- 1 egg
- 1 spoon of fresh parsley leaves, chopped
- 1 garlic clove
- 2 spoons of almond flour
- 1 teaspoon of coconut flour
- 1 avocado
- 1-2 teaspoons of lemon juice
- ¼ cup of valerian leaves for décor
- 2 spoons of ghee or coconut oil for frying
- salt, pepper and paprika to taste
- cayenne pepper-optional, for décor

Preparation

Mince the chicken breast in the food processor together with the garlic and the parsley leaves. Mix it in a bowl with the egg, the almond flour, coconut flour and the condiments.

Make 3 mini patties by hand and fry them in ghee or coconut oil, at medium heat.

In the meantime, mash the avocado with a fork and add a little salt and the lemon juice to it.

Fry the mushroom separately for as long as they leave a bit of water but are still hard-around 5 minutes, on low heat.

Combine all the ingredients and put together the mini burgers: use the mushrooms as a bun, add the ckicken patties, the valerian leaves, and the mashed avocado on top.

Sprinkle a little bit of cayenne pepper and serve.

Note: the chicken patties can be made in big batches and freeze. This way you could put together a healthy breakfast in just 5 minutes.

Egg and greens bowl

Ingredients

- 4 slices of crunchy fried bacon, chopped
- 1 egg, boiled soft-for about 6 minutes
- half an avocado, sliced
- 2 thin spring onions
- 1 cup of valerian leaves, fresh
- 1 cup of rucola leaves, fresh
- ½ cup of lettuce leaves
- a pinch of salt (pay attention if the bacon is salty)

For the vinaigrette

- 1 spoon of lemon juice
- 1 spoon of olive oil

Preparation

Wash the greens and mix them in a salad bowl with the chopped spring onions. Add the avocado, the egg cut in half and the chopped bacon. Season with a little salt and pepper and pour the vinaigrette on top.

Kale and mushroom frittata

Ingredients

- 8 eggs
- 2 spring onions, chopped
- 5 champignon (white button) mushrooms, chopped
- 5 kale leaves
- 1 cup of broccoli florets
- 1 garlic clove, crushed
- 2 spoons of ghee
- ½ teaspoon of naturally smoked paprika
- salt and pepper to taste

Preparation

Sauté the onions, broccoli, mushrooms, and garlic in a heated pan, at medium heat, with a spoon of ghee.

Wash the kale leaves and cut their stems off. Boil them for 5-10 minutes in a pot with water and salt. Take them out and cut them into smaller pieces.

Add the cut kale leaves to the sautéed vegetables, together with the other spoon of ghee and mix well.

Beat the eggs with salt, pepper and paprika and pour them over the mixed vegetables. Cook them for about 5 minutes, at low heat and then move the dish in the oven where you bake them for another 10 minutes, at medium heat (176°C or 350°F).

Remove and serve as soon as it is cool enough to eat.

Granola

Ingredients

- 1/3 cup of Brazil nuts (around 10-11 nuts), chopped small
- ¼ cup of chopped almonds
- ½ cup of big coconut flakes
- ½ cup of almond flakes
- 1 spoons of raw honey
- ¼ teaspoon of Madagascar vanilla powder

Preparation

Mix the honey with all the ingredients, except for the almond flakes that we leave aside for now. Put the composition you obtained on a tray prepared with baking paper and bake in the oven at low heat (65°C or 150°F), for about 10-15 minutes. Make sure to check and turn the compositon to the other side every 5 minutes so it does not burn.

When it is baked and ready, add the almond flakes and the vanilla powder. Mix and let it cool. Store in a closed container, hermetically sealed.

Bacon, spinach, and green onion waffles

Ingredients

- 1 and a half cups of almond flour
- ¼ cup of coconut flour
- 6 eggs
- 1 cup of coconut cream
- 3 slices of crispy bacon, chopped (1/2 cup)
- 3 spring onions, chopped
- ½ cup of baby spinach, chopped
- ¼ teaspoon of Himalayan salt (pay attention to how salty the bacon is)

Preparation

Mix the all the ingredients in a bowl, with a whisk-the eggs and coconut cream first, then add the dry ingredients and then mix in the bacon, onions, and the spinach.

Pour in the waffle maker and cook until ready.

From this dough you make 6 big waffles, in a waffle machine that is the size of 10/8 cm (4x3 inches).

Nutritious raspberry bowl

Ingredients

- 1 well ripened banana, with dark spots on
- ½ cup of fresh or frozen raspberry
- 1 spoon of coconut butter
- 2 spoons of almond butter
- 1 spoon of chopped pistachio

Preparation

Put the banana, raspberry and butters in the food processor and mix until they turn into a beautiful cream. Pour this in a bowl and sprinkle the chopped pistachio on top. Serve fresh.

Vegetable egg muffins

Ingredients

- 4 eggs
- 4 slices of bacon
- ½ red pepper, chopped
- 1 cup of fresh baby spinach
- 1 spring onion

Preparation

Fry the bacon slices in a heated pan, at medium heat, until they become crisp. Remove them on a plate and sauté the onion and the pepper in the fat that is left in the pan. When they become soft and tend to change color, add the baby spinach, and leave to cook for another minute.

Cut the bacon in small pieces.

Beat the eggs, mix everything, and pour in the muffin tin. Bake for 20 minutes, in the preheated oven, at medium heat, (176°C or 350°F).

Out of this composition you make 6 regular size muffins.

"Porridge"

Ingredients

- ½ cup of Cajun nuts
- 2 seedless dates
- 1 banana
- 1 spoon of granola (page 18)
- ¼ teaspoon of Madagascar vanilla powder
- ½ cup of coconut cream
- 1 spoon of raisins, sugar-free
- 1 spoon of dried cranberries, sugar-free

Preparation

Leave the Cajun nuts and dates to soak in warm water for 30 minutes or in cold water from evening to morning. Place them in the food processor, add the vanilla powder and coconut cream and blend well.

Pour everything in a bowl. Add manually the raisins and the cranberries and mix with a spoon.

Pour granola on top and serve immediately.

Fruit "porridge"

Ingredients (serves two)

- ½ cup of soaked Cajun nuts
- 1/3 cup of almond granules
- 1 well ripened banana, sliced
- ¼ cup of fresh blueberries
- ¼ cup of fresh raspberries
- ¼ cup of hemp seeds
- ¼ cup of coconut cream
- 1 traspoon of vanilla essence
- 1 teaspoon of raw honey
- 1 spoon of coconut flakes

Preparation

Put the coconut cream, vanilla, honey and nuts in the food processor and blend well. Add the almonds granules and mix by hand, with a spoon.

Pour the mixture in a bowl and add the sliced banana, blueberries, raspberries, and coconut flakes.

Serve fresh.

Salad roll with eggs and bacon

Ingredients

- 4-5 slices of bacon
- 2 scrambled eggs
- 5-6 thin slices of red pepper
- 4-5 leaves of iceberg salad
- 1 sheet of baking paper

Preparation

Place the lettuce leaves on a piece of parchment paper in such a way that you have free edges on the sides.

Put all the other ingredients on the leaves and wrap around using the paper as support.

Cut into two with a sharp knife and serve.

They can be easily packed to go.

Stuffed avocado

Ingredients

- 1 avocado
- 1 yellow pepper
- 1 cup of diced chicken breast
- ½ cup of cherry tomatoes, cut in half (6-7 pieces)
- 1 spoon of chopped fresh parsley leaves
- ½ spoon of lemon juice
- 2 spoons of mayonnaise (page 123)
- ¼ teaspoon garlic powder
- ¼ teaspoon of dried oregano
- ¼ teaspoon of paprika
- 1 spoon of ghee or coconut oil
- salt and pepper to taste

Preparation

Season the chicken with salt, pepper, garlic powder, oregano and pepper and fry in a heated pan, at medium heat, with coconut oil or ghee.

Clean and cube out the avocado.

Mix all the ingredients in a bowl and sprinkle with lemon juice. Serve with mayonnaise and green parsley on top.

It can even be served in its own avocado shell.

Pancakes with spinach and boletus mushrooms

Ingredients (for 7 large pancakes)

For the dough

- 2 cups of fresh baby spinach
- 3 eggs
- ½ teaspoon of Himalayan salt
- ½ teaspoon of garlic powder
- ¼ cup of still water
- coconut oil for frying

For the stuffing

- 4 cups of boletus mushrooms, cut into small cubes
- 1 garlic clove or ¼ teaspoon of garlic powder
- 1 teaspoon of fresh parsley leaves, chopped
- 1 spoon of ghee

Preparation

Put all the ingredients for the dough in the food processor and mix them well.

Cook the dough in a heated pancake pan, at medium heat. Make sure you use a good quality pan and a good quality spatula, thin and flexible, to be able to turn over the pancakes easily in the pan.

Sauté the mushrooms with the garlic, at medium heat, with the spoon of ghee, in a different frying pan.

To build, place the stuffing over the pancakes and roll. Add salt to taste and the freshly chopped parsley leaves on top.

Crêpes, French pancakes, with mushrooms and white sauce

Ingredients

For the dough

- 6 egg whites
- 1 spoon of coconut flour
- salt and white pepper to taste-about a pinch each

For the stuffing

- 1 and a half cup of white button mushrooms, chopped
- 2 garlic cloves
- ½ teaspoon of fresh parsley leaves, chopped
- ½ cup of soaked Cajun nuts (soak them in warm water for 30 minutes or in cold water overnight)
- 1 spoon of ghee or coconut oil

Preparation

Beat the egg whites with the coconut flour, salt, and pepper.

In a heated pancake pan pour the dough in a very thin layer. Cook at low to medium heat. Spread it and turn it over slowly with a flexilble spatula. Be careful, the dough is sensitive, and it will break if you do not allow it to cook completely and you try to turn it over before it is ready.

Sauté the mushrooms with the garlic and a spoon of ghee or coconut oil in a heated pan, at medium heat.

Remove the Cajun nuts from the water, add them to the food processor with a spoon of water and mix them until they become creamy. Add them over the mushrooms with the parsley and mix everything well.

Place the pancakes on a big plate. Add one stuffing spoon, fold them and serve warm.

Note: From this mixture you can make 3 big crêpes.

Almond pancakes with strawberry sauce

Ingredients

For the dough

- 1 cup of almond flour
- 2 spoons of coconut flour
- 1 spoon of raw honey
- ¼ teaspoon of Madagascar vanilla powder
- ½ teaspoon of vanilla essence
- 3 eggs
- ½ cup of sparkling water
- coconut oil for frying

For the strawberry sauce

- 2 cups of fresh strawberries
- 2 spoons of raw honey

Preparation

Mix all the dough ingredients in a bowl, with a whisk. The dough will be runny, so you need to scoop it out.

Cook them one by one in a hot frying pan, at medium heat, with a little coconut oil.

Add all the ingredients for the sauce in a different dish and crush them with your fingers. Mix everything using your hand.

Serve the pancakes warm, with the strawberry sauce and with chopped almonds on top if you would like.

Coconut blueberry pancakes

Ingredients

- ½ cup of coconut flour
- ½ cup of coconut cream
- ½ spoon of raw honey
- 3 eggs
- 1 cup of sparkling water
- ½ cup of blueberries (fresh or frozen)
- ½ spoon of fresh lemon zest
- ½ cup of fine coconut flakes
- coconut oil for frying

Preparation

Except for the blueberries, put all the other ingredients in the food processor and mix well. Add the blueberries with a spoon and incorporate manually.

Cook them in a hot frying pan, at medium heat, with some coconut oil.

You need to make small pancakes because the dough is sensitive, and it can break until is cooked on both sides. Use a thin and flexible spatula and turn the pancakes over carefully.

Mug cake

Ingredients

- 1 cup of almond flour
- ¼ cup of coconut flour
- ½ teaspoon of baking soda (aluminum free)
- 2 spoons of raw honey
- 4 eggs
- ¼ cup of ghee
- ½ cup of coconut milk
- 1 cup of berries

Preparation

Except for the berries, mix all the ingredients in a food processor or manually with a whisk. Incorporate the berries into the dough with a spoon.

Pour in 4 small ramenkins and bake in the oven, at medium heat (176°C or 350°F), for 20 minutes.

Morning Glory muffins

Ingredients

- 2 cups of almond flour
- ½ teaspoon of baking soda (aluminum-free)
- ¼ cup of raw honey
- 2 eggs
- ½ cup of apple sauce
- 1 cup of a finely grated carrot
- ½ cup of raisins (sugar-free)
- ½ cup of finely chopped walnuts
- ½ teaspoon of nutmeg powder
- 1 teaspoon of cinnamon
- ½ teaspoon of ginger powder

Preparation

Mix the almond flour, sodium bicarbonate, honey, eggs, and apple sauce in a bowl, with a whisk, or in the food processor.

Incorporate all the other ingredients manually. The dough will be dense, so you need to spoon it in the muffin tin.

Cook for 30 minutes in the preheated oven, at medium heat (176°C or 350°F).

From this composition you will make 12 regular size muffins.

Nutritious breakfast bowl

Ingredients

- 2 spoons of organic peanut butter
- 1 well ripened banana, with dark spots on
- 2 eggs
- ½ an apple
- 1 spoon of coconut oil for frying

For the sauce:

- 1 spoon of peanut butter
- 2 teaspoons of honey
- 2 teaspoons of ghee

Preparation

Beat the eggs together with the peanut butter and the banana and fry them in a heated pan, at medium heat, with coconut oil. Scramble them up in the pan, like you would make scrambled eggs.

Once cooked, place them in a bowl. Cut the apple in small pieces and sprinkle on top.

Mix all the ingredientes for the sauce and pour on top. Serve immediately.

Pumpkin and sun-dried tomato waffles

Ingredients

- 2 cups of almond flour
- 1 spoon of coconut flour
- ½ cup of pumpkin purée
- 7 eggs
- ¼ cup of sun-dried tomatoes, sliced small
- 1 spoon of chopped chives
- ½ teaspoon of dried oregano
- ½ teaspoon of Himalayan salt
- ½ teaspoon of garlic powder
- ½ teaspoon of ginger powder
- ¼ teaspoon of white pepper powder
- 1 spoon of onion flakes

Preparation

Put the flours in a bowl and mix with a whisk. Add the rest of the ingredients and incorporate until you have the dough.

Pour in the waffle maker and cook. Serve warm.

From this dough I made 6 big waffles, from a size 10/8cm (4x3 inches) waffle maker.

Savoury zucchini and bacon muffins

Ingredients

- 1 grated zucchini, squeezed to remove excess water
- 1 cup and a half of almond flour
- ¼ cup of coconut flour
- 4 eggs
- 1 cup of coconut cream
- 1 teaspoon of garlic powder
- 2 spoons of chives, chopped
- 3 crispy bacon slices, chopped
- ¼ teaspoon of Himalayan salt (pay attention to how salty the bacon is)
- ½ teaspoon of baking soda, aluminum-free

Preparation

Mix the flours in a bowl with a whisk.

Cook the bacon in a frying pan on low heat, until it becomes crunchy. Then chop in small pieces.

Add all rest of the ingredients into the bowl with the flours and incorporate manually to make the dough.

Spoon in the muffin tins and cook in the preheated oven, at medium heat (176°C or 350°F), for 25 minutes or until a toothpick would come out dry when you poke them in the middle.

From this recipe you can make 14 medium size muffins.

Blueberry Danish breakfast casserole

Ingredients

For the dough

- ½ cup of coconut flour
- ½ teaspoon of baking soda, aluminum-free
- 2 spoons of coconut oil
- 1 spoon of raw honey
- 3 eggs
- ½ cup of coconut cream
- ½ teaspoon of vanilla essence

For the topping

- 1 cup of coconut cream, separated into two
- 1 spoon of water
- 1 spoon of raw honey
- ¼ teaspoon of Madagascar vanilla powder
- 1 cup of blueberries (fresh or frozen)

Preparation

Mix all the ingredients for the dough in the food processor or in a bowl, with a whisk. Pour the dough in a baking dish prepared with parchment paper, with a diameter of approximately 20 cm, 20 cm length, 14 cm width and 5 cm height.

Cook at medium heat (176°C or 350°F) in the preheated oven, for 15-20 minutes or until the toothpick you insert in the middle comes out clean.

Let it cool and then cut into cubes. Remove the baking paper from the dish and add back the now cut and cooked danish with the blueberries.

Mix half the coconut cream with the honey, vanilla powder and the spoon of water and pour over. Place it back to the oven and cook for another 5 minutes, at medium heat.

Then pour the other half of coconut cream on top. Serve as soon as it is cool enough to eat.

Egg and vegetable Shakshuka (Russian breakfast)

Ingredients

- 1 white onion, chopped
- 1 red pepper, diced
- 2 tomatoes, diced
- 2 garlic cloves, chopped
- ½ teaspoon of Himalayan salt
- ¼ teaspoon of black pepper powder
- ¼ teaspoon of turmeric powder
- ¼ teaspoon of cumin powder
- ¼ teaspoon of ginger powder
- 1 spoon of olive oil
- 3 or 4 eggs
- some parsley leaves for décor

Preparation

Sauté the onion and the pepper with the spoon of olive oil, then add the tomatoes and the garlic and cook together at medium heat until all the vegetables are tender. Add all the condiments and mix well.

Make a little room with a spoon, like a nest between the vegetables. Break the eggs in the spaces you created and let them cook with a lid on, at low heat, for 5 minutes.

Pour some parsley leaves on top and move the dish into the oven for another 5 minutes, at medium heat (176°C or 350°F).

Serve immediately.

Walnut and banana muffins

Ingredients

- ½ cup of fine ground walnuts
- ¼ cup of coconut flour
- ½ teaspoon of aluminum-free baking soda
- 3 eggs
- 2 well ripened bananas, with dark spots on
- 1 spoon of raw honey
- 2 spoons of half walnuts for décor

Preparation

Except for the décor walnuts, mix all ingredients in a food processor to make the dough.

Pour in the muffin molds and add half a walnut on top.

Bake in the preheated oven, at medium heat (176°C or 350°F), for 25 minutes or until the toothpick comes clean when inserted in the middle.

"Oatmeal" breakfast bowl

Ingredients

- ½ cup of almonds, soaked in hot water for 30 minutes
- 2 dates, soaked in hot water for 30 minutes
- ¼ cup of coconut flakes
- 1 well ripened banana, with dark spots on
- ¼ teaspoon of cinnamon powder
- 1 apple, diced
- 2 spoons of almond milk
- 1 spoon of almond butter

Preparation

If almonds have the skin on, remove them after soaking. Place them in the food processor with the dates, the banana, cinnamon, and the almond milk.

Pulse until the mixture ends up having a texture like the oats.

Add the pieces of apple and coconut flakes and mix manually in a bowl.

Pour the almond butter on top and serve.

Red beet almond pancakes

Ingredients

- 1 small fresh red beet, grated
- 1 cup of almond flour
- 4 eggs
- ½ spoon of coconut flour
- ½ teaspoon of Himalayan salt
- ¼ teaspoon of cumin powder
- ¼ teaspoon of garlic powder
- coconut oil for frying

Preparation

Place all the dry ingredients in a bowl and mix well with a whisk. Add the eggs and the red beet and incorporate in the dough.

Heat a frying pan with the coconut oil and cook them at medium heat.

Make these pancakes small, with a diameter of around 10 cm (about 4 inches) so you can turn them over easily with a flexible spatula.

Out of this dough you will make 6 pancakes of this size.

Breakfast tart

Ingredients

- 1 piece of fresh homemade sausage (10 cm long) or 65 grams of minced porc
- 3 eggs
- 2 spring onions, chopped
- 5 slices of sun-dried tomatoes, chopped
- 1 cup of fresh baby spinach, chopped
- 1 spoon of olive oil for sautéing
- salt and pepper to taste

For the dough

- 1 cup of almond flour
- 1 spoon of coconut flour
- 1 spoon of onion flakes
- ½ teaspoon of Himalayan salt
- 1 egg
- ¼ cup of melted ghee

Preparation

To prepare the dough place all the dry ingredients in the food processor and pulse a few times. Then add the rest of the ingredients and mix well, until you see the texture becomes dense, turning into a ball as it spins.

Divide in two, place on a piece of parchment paper and leave for 10 minutes in the refrigerator.

You can use half for this type of recipe and half for the recipe on the following page or simply store in the freezer for later use. If you want to make 4 tarts or a bigger tart, double the ingredients for the composition.

Meanwhile, prepare the filling. Cook the spring onions and the porc in a frying pan with the olive oil, at medium heat. Add the sun-dried tomatoes. When the meat and the onions are cooked, remove the pan from the fire and add the spinach, mixing carefully to incorportate. Add salt and pepper to taste and leave on the side.

Beat the eggs with a pinch of salt and black pepper in a separate bowl.

Remove the dough from the fridge and roll between two sheets of parchment paper. Then place and mold with your fingers in two separate ramekins with a 12 cm (about 4.7 inches) diameter.

Add the eggs to the filling, incorporate well and pour over the dough, in the two dishes.

Cook in the preheated oven, at medium heat (176°C or 350°F), for 10-12 minutes.

Note: The dough can be prepared in the evening with part of the filling and stored in the refrigerator. Just beat the eggs in the morning and breakfast is ready in 10 minutes.

Kale and peas tart

Ingredients

- 4 eggs
- 2 slices of bacon, chopped (about ¼ of a cup)
- 2 spring onions, chopped
- 2 kale leaves, chopped and stems removed
- ¼ cup of peas plus 1 spoon
- 2 garlic cloves, chopped
- salt and pepper to taste

For the dough

- 1 cup of almond flour
- 1 spoon of coconut flour
- 1 spoon of onion flakes
- ½ teaspoon of Himalayan salt
- 1 egg
- ¼ cup of melted ghee

Preparation

To prepare the dough place all the dry ingredients in the food processor and pulse a few times. Then add the rest of the ingredients and mix well, until you see the texture becomes dense, turning into a ball as it spins.

Divide in two, place on a piece of parchment paper and leave for 10 minutes in the refrigerator.

You can use half for this type of recipe and half for the previous recipe or store in the freezer for later use. If you want to make 4 tarts or a bigger tart, double the ingredients for the composition.

Meanwhile, prepare the stuffing. Heat a frying pan over the fire and cook the bacon at medium heat, until it becomes crispy and leaves the fat in the pan. Add the onions, the kale leaves, the peas, and the garlic in that fat. Let them cook, lid on, until they become tender and the onion changes color. Remove from the fire and let them cool a little.

Beat the eggs in a bowl with salt and pepper.

Remove the dough from the fridge and roll between two sheets of parchment paper. Then place and mold with your fingers in two separate ramekins with a 12 cm (about 4.7 inches) diameter.

Add the eggs to the filling, incorporate well and pour over the dough, in the two dishes.

Cook in the preheated oven, at medium heat (176°C or 350°F), for 10-12 minutes.

Note: The dough can be prepared in the evening with part of the filling and stored in the refrigerator. Just beat the eggs in the morning and breakfast is ready in 10 minutes.

Lemon chicken thighs with artichokes and sun-dried tomatoes

Ingredients

- 6 big chicken thighs, skin, and bone on
- ½ teaspoon of dried thyme
- 1 teaspoon of dried oregano
- 4 garlic cloves, sliced
- 1 big white onion, chopped
- 1 cup of sun-dried tomatoes, halves
- 1 cup of artichokes from the jar, cut into small pieces
- 1 spoon of capers
- ½ lemon, sliced
- juice from half a lemon
- ½ cup of ghee
- 2 cups of still water
- salt, pepper and paprika to taste

Preparation

Marinate the thighs with salt, pepper and paprika. Place them in a dish prepared for the oven in which you add all the other ingredients, except the lemon and artichokes.

Leave in the oven at medium heat (176°C or 350°F) for 40 minutes, lid on. Then remove the lid, add the artichokes, lemon juice and lemon slices and leave in the oven for another 20 minutes, at medium heat.

Serve with your favorite side dish or with cauliflower purée.

One pot "rice" and vegetables

Ingredients

- 1 medium size riced cauliflower
- 4 medium size champignon mushrooms, diced
- 1 cup of broccoli florets, chopped
- 1 red pepper, medium size, diced
- 1 medium size carrot, sliced thin
- 3 spring onions, sliced
- 4 garlic cloves, sliced
- 2 full chicken thighs, baked in the oven, skin and bone removed and chopped
- 1 spoon of sesame seeds (optional)
- 2 spoons of coconut oil or ghee
- salt, pepper, and turmeric to taste

Preparation

Fry the carrot with the mushrooms and the two spoons of ghee or coconut oil for 10 minutes, at medium heat, lid on. Add the rest of the vegetables except for the riced cauliflower and cook for another 10-15 minutes. Add the riced cauliflower, the chicken, spices, and sesame seeds and cook for another 5 minutes, at low heat.

Be careful that the "rice" does not overcook and becomes too soft.

Sprinkle the chopped leaves of the spring onions on top and serve immediately.

Stuffed peppers

Ingredients

- 8-10 white bell peppers, depending on size
- 500 grams of pork pulp, minced
- 1 cup and a half of celery root, grated big
- 1 white onion, diced
- 4 garlic cloves, sliced
- 2 cups of tomato purée
- 1 cup of bacon, cut in small and thin slices
- 1 teaspoon of dried thyme leaves
- salt, pepper, and turmeric to taste
- 1 spoon of lard (or coconut oil) for frying

Preparation

Fry the bacon in a preheated pan, at medium heat, until it becomes crispy and releases the fat. In the same pan, sauté the onion, garlic, and celery in the lard until the onion becomes translucent, over low heat, stirring constantly.

Then add the meat and mix until it changes color.

Pour over 1 cup of tomato purée and sprinkle the thyme leaves on top.

Fill the peppers with the mixture and place them in an oven dish. Pour the other cup of tomato purée over them and cook in the preheated oven, at medium heat (176°C or 350°F), for an hour.

Sour pork with vegetables

Ingredients

- 3 cups of pork, cut into small cubes
- 2 cups of green beans, halved
- 4 cups of small broccoli florets
- 1 red bell pepper, sliced
- 2 white onions, medium size, chopped
- 4 garlic cloves, chopped
- 1 spoon of ghee or coconut oil for frying
- 1 teaspoon of turmeric
- 1 teaspoon of paprika
- 1 teaspoon of cumin powder
- 2-3 spoons of still water
- 2 spoons of lemon juice, freshly squeezed
- salt and pepper to taste

Preparation

Sauté the onion in a heated pan with the spoon of ghee or coconut oil, at medium heat, until it becomes translucent.

Add the meat and cook at low heat, lid on, for 10-15 minutes until it changes color well and it crusts. Then add the garlic, beans, broccoli, and pepper. Sprinkle all the spices and water and let everything cook with the lid on, at low heat for about 25 minutes or longer.

Once ready, remove from the heat and sprinkle the lemon juice. Stir well and serve.

Homemade chicken cremwurst or pork sausage with vegetables

Ingredients

- 6 cremwurst (recipe on the blog or on page 127) or homemade sausage, sliced
- 1 white onion, chopped
- 4 spring onions, sliced
- 1 zucchini, cut into small pieces
- 1 red bell pepper, cut into small pieces
- 2 garlic cloves, chopped
- 4 pieces of asparagus, cut into small pieces
- 3 spoons of fresh lemon juice
- 2 spoons of olive oil
- 1 spoon of green parsley leaves, chopped
- salt and pepper to taste

Preparation

Sauté the onion with the red pepper in a heated pan, at medium heat, with the spoon of ghee until they change color and become softer. Add the garlic, zucchini, the green onions, and the sausage slices.

Cook together, lid on, for another 5-7 minutes, at medium heat. Put the pieces of asparagus on top, lid on, and cook in the steam and heat from the food for another 2-3 minutes, at low heat.

Sprinkle salt, pepper, add the lemon juice, parsley and olive oil and serve.

Pork with mushrooms

Ingredients

- 650 grams of pork shoulder, no bone, sliced
- 2 white onions, chopped
- 4 garlic cloves
- 3 cups of boletus mushrooms, diced
- 2 cups of honey mushrooms (or any mushrooms of choice)
- 1 spoon of coriander seeds
- 1 spoon of dried thyme
- 1 spoon of garlic flakes
- salt, pepper and paprika to marinate
- 1 spoon of ghee, to sauté
- 1 cup of water
- 1 bunch of fresh parsley leaves, chopped (1/4 cup)
- ½ cup of dried yeast (optional, not during the first 6 months of the diet)

Preparation

Marinate the meat with salt, pepper and paprika and set aside for 25 minutes.

Sauté the onion in a heated frying pan with the spoon of ghee, at medium heat, until it becomes translucent.

Fry the slices of meat on both sides until crusty. Add the garlic, both fresh and the flakes, the mushrooms, spices, and the cup of water. Let them cook on low heat, lid on, for about 40 minutes. If need be or if you like more gravy add more water as it cooks.

When ready, sprinkle the parsley and the dried yeast (if tolerated) on top.

Serve with cauliflower purée or with the favorite vegetables.

Coconut cream lemon chicken

Ingredients

- 5 chicken thighs, skin, and bone on
- 1 onion, chopped
- 4 garlic cloves, crushed
- 1 big tomato, diced
- salt, pepper and paprika to taste
- 1 spoon of lemon juice
- 1 teaspoon of turmeric
- 1 cup of coconut cream
- 1 cup of water
- 1 spoon of freshly chopped parsley leaves
- 2 spoons of coconut oil

Preparation

Season the chicken thighs with salt, pepper and lemon juice and cover for 20 minutes.

Fry them in a heated pan with the two spoons of coconut oil, at medium heat, with the lid on, for about 20 minutes, turning them on both sides repeatedly.

Add the onion and let them cook a bit longer, lid on, until the onion changes color. Then add the remaining ingredients and cook for another 45 minutes, at low heat.

Sprinkle the fresh parsley on top when they are cooked and remove from the heat.

Serve with cauliflower, parsnip, or celery root purée.

Cajun chicken with zucchini noodles

Ingredients

- 1 chicken breast, cut into small cubes
- 1 white onion, chopped
- 2 garlic cloves, crushed
- 1 red bell pepper, sliced on the length
- ½ spoon of fresh parsley leaves, chopped
- 1 zucchini, spiralized
- 1 cup of small broccoli florets
- 2 spoons of coconut oil or ghee
- ¼ cup of Cajun nuts, chopped and roasted
- optional-a small chilli pepper

For the sauce:

- ½ cup of Cajun nuts, soaked in cold water from evening to morning or in hot water for 30 minutes
- 1-2 spoons of lemon juice
- ½ cup of water
- ¼ teaspoon of sea salt

Preparation

Fry the chicken in a heated pan with the onion, garlic, and broccoli, at medium heat, for about 15 minutes or until ready.

Cook the red pepper separately, in a pan with a little ghee or in the oven, until it becomes soft.

Season everything with salt and pepper.

Put all the ingredients for the sauce in the food processor and mix until you get a texture like thick sour cream. Pour over the ingredients in the pan and mix well.

Heat up the zucchini noodles in another pan with a bit of ghee, until they soften a little-for about 3 minutes. Add them to the chicken, vegetables and sauce and incorporate well.

Move them to a bowl with the red bell pepper slices and optionally a few slices of lemon. Sprinkle the roasted Cajun nuts on top and the chopped chilli pepper if you prefer it and serve.

Vegetable and pork stew

Ingredients

- 500 grams of pork, cut into cubes
- 1 big yellow bell pepper or 2 smaller yellow peppers
- 2 cups of broccoli florets
- 1 cup and a half of celery root, grated
- 1 white onion, chopped
- 3 garlic cloves, crushed
- ½ cup of tomato purée
- ½ cup of coconut cream
- 1 teaspoon of mustard seeds
- 2 teaspoons of curry
- 1 teaspoon of turmeric
- 1 teaspoon of dry oregano leaves
- ½ teaspoon of chilli powder
- 1 teaspoon of dry basil leaves
- salt and pepper to taste
- 1 bay leaf
- ½ spoon of dry marjoram leaves
- 2 spoons of coconut oil
- 4 cups of still water

Preparation

Season the meat with salt and pepper and set aside for about 20 minutes. Then fry it in a preheated pan, at medium heat, with the coconut oil, until it gets crusty on all sides. Add the onion, garlic, pepper, broccoli, and sauté a little with the lid on, until the onion begins to change its color and the pepper begins to soften.

Add the rest of the ingredients and cook at low heat for another 30 minutes. Serve with cauliflower rice or on its own.

Pork and bacon medallions

Ingredients

- 7 pieces of pork with a diameter of 5-6 cm (about 2.3 inches) and thickness of 2 cm (under 1 inch)
- 7 slices of bacon
- 1 spoon of ghee
- ½ teaspoon of thyme
- ½ teaspoon of marjoram
- salt, pepper and paprika to taste

Preparation

Season the meat with salt, pepper and paprika.

Cook the slices of bacon on a tray in the preheated oven, at medium heat (176°C or 350°F) until they become tender and soft. Then wrap the meat pieces with the bacon slices and close them on the side with a toothpick.

Fry them in a preheated pan, with the spoon of ghee, at medium heat, until they get a crust on a side. Then turn them over. Sprinkle the rest of the ingredients and add a bit of water to the pan. Let them cook at low heat, lid on, until the meat if fully cooked, about 30 minutes.

Serve with the favorite vegetables.

Pork tenderloin with aromatic herbs

Ingredients

- 1 piece of pork tenderloin of about 600 grams
- 6 garlic cloves, chopped
- ½ teaspoon of fresh thyme leaves
- ½ teaspoon of marjoram leaves
- ½ teaspoon of rosemary leaves
- ½ teaspoon of sage, powder
- salt, pepper and paprika to taste
- 1 spoon of ghee

Preparation

Add all spices in a bowl with the garlic. Mix well and season the entire tenderloin piece. Use your fingers and rub the spices all over the meat.

Fry the meat in a preheated pan, at medium heat, until it makes a crust-around 2-3 minutes. Then add a cup of still water and bake in the oven, lid on, at medium heat (176°C or 350°F), for another 30-35 minutes.

Serve with cauliflower purée or with the favorite vegetables.

Oven-baked Fajitas

Ingredients

- 1 chicken breast, cut into long slices
- 1 red bell pepper, cut into long slices
- 1 yellow bell pepper, cut into long slices
- 1 green pepper, cut into long slices
- 1 white onion, sliced julienne
- 1 red onion, sliced julienne
- 1 teaspoon of salt
- ½ teaspoon of black pepper
- ½ teaspoon of white pepper
- 1 teaspoon of smoked paprika
- 1 teaspoon of garlic powder
- 1 teaspoon of onion flakes
- 1 teaspoon of cumin powder
- 1 teaspoon of dry oregano
- 1 teaspoon of dry basil
- 1 teaspoon of dry marjoram
- 1 teaspoon of chilli powder-optional
- 1 teaspoon of turmeric powder-optional
- 2 spoons of ghee
- 1 spoon of parsley leaves, freshly chopped
- the juice from one lime

Preparation

Mix all condiments in a bowl. Then pour the melted ghee on top and add all the other ingredients except for the parsley leaves and the lime juice.

Mix everything well and bake in the preheated oven, at medium heat (176°C or 350°F) for about 20-30 minutes.

Remove the tray from the oven, sprinkle the parsley leaves and pour the lime juice on top. Serve on lettuce leaves or in pita bread, recipe to follow.

Teriyaki Chicken

Ingredients

- 1 chicken breast, sliced long
- 1 broccoli, small florets
- 2 big carrots, sliced
- 3 small carrots, thin, long slices
- 2 white onions, sliced
- 5 garlic cloves, chopped
- 1 cup of small pineapple pieces (optional but great addition to taste)
- 1 teaspoon of Himalayan salt
- ½ teaspoon of black pepper
- 2 spoons of honey
- 2 spoons of apple cider vinegar
- 1 teaspoon of smoked paprika
- 2 spoons of ghee, melted

Preparation

Mix the salt, pepper, honey, vinegar, paprika and garlic and season the chicken and vegetables with the mixture.

Bake them in the preheated oven, at medium heat (176°C or 350°F), for around 20-30 minutes.

Serve as is or with cauliflower rice.

Nutritious bowl with chicken and vegetables

Ingredients

- ½ pumpkin or 1 smaller pumpkin, cleaned and sliced
- 2 cups of broccoli, small florets
- 1 chicken breast, sliced
- 1 cup of mixed greens
- 1 spoon of ghee or coconut oil
- 1 teaspoon of pine nuts
- 1 spoon of olive oil
- 1 spoon of lemon juice or apple cider vinegar
- salt and pepper to taste

Preparation

Season the pumpkin with a bit of salt and bake in the preheated oven for about one hour, at medium heat (176°C or 350°F). Once it cools a bit cut it into small cubes.

Sauté the broccoli florets in a heated pan with a little ghee or coconut oil and season with salt and pepper.

Season the chiken breast as well with salt and pepper and cook on a grill, in a frying pan or in the oven, depending on preferences and your time. Once cooked, cut into smaller pieces.

Wash the mixed greens, sprinkle salt, and pour the lemon juice or apple cider vinegar on top.

Build the bowl by adding the mixed greens to the broccoli, pumpkin and chicken breast.

Sprinkle the pine nuts over and serve.

Chicken with asparagus, broccoli, and cherry tomatoes

Ingredients

- 1 chicken breast
- 1 spoon of ghee or coconut oil
- 1 cup and a half of cherry tomatoes
- 1 cup of small broccoli florets
- 1 garlic clove
- 10 pieces of asparagus
- 1 teaspoon of green parsley, freshly chopped

Preparation

Cut the chicken breast into smaller pieces and fry in a heated pan, at medium heat, with the spoon of ghee or coconut oil, with the chopped garlic.

When the chicken is browning add the broccoli, tomatoes and the asparagus and cook at low heat for about 10 minutes.

Sprinkle the green parsley on top and serve.

Chicken skewers with salad and refreshing sour sauce

Ingredients

- ½ chicken breast, cut into small pieces
- 1 cup of sliced cucumbers
- 1 cup of white cabbage, sliced thin
- ½ teaspoon of Himalayan salt
- ¼ teaspoon of black pepper
- ½ teaspoon of paprika
- 1 teaspoon of dried oregano leaves
- ½ teaspoon of lemon juice
- 1 spoon of olive oil, plus another half a spoon for the salad
- 1 teaspoon of apple cider vinegar for the salad

For the sauce:
- ½ cup of Cajun nuts, soaked in water
- ½ an avocado
- ¼ cup of still water
- 1 spoon of green dill, chopped
- 1 spoon and a half of lemon juice
- ½ teaspoon of Himalayan salt

Preparation

Season the chicken pieces with salt, papper, paprika, oregano, the half spoon of lemon juice and one spoon of olive oil. Let them marinate for 20 minutes.

Prepare 4-5 bamboo or wooden skewers and leave them soaking in water during all this time.

Then skewer the chicken and cook it on a greased grill or in a preheated pan, at medium heat.

Cut the cabbage and the cucumbers and season with olive oil, apple cider vinegar, salt, and pepper to taste.

To make the sauce add all ingredients in the food processor or in a blender and blend well. Serve fresh.

Pesto chicken with cherry tomatoes on lettuce leaves

Ingredients

- 1 chicken breast
- 1 cup of cherry tomatoes, halved
- 1 spoon of ghee
- 1 white onion, chopped
- ½ cup of tomato purée
- ½ cup of water
- ½ spoon of fresh basil leaves, chopped
- 1 bay leaf
- ¼ cup of basil leaves, blended with a little water until they become a paste
- salt, pepper and paprika to taste
- 6-7 salad leaves

Preparation

Season the chicken breast with salt, pepper and paprika and fry with the ghee in a preheated pan, at medium heat, until crusty. Add the onion until it changes color and becomes a bit translucent. Then add the tomatoes, water, and bay leaf. Cook at medium heat, lid on, until ready.

Sprinkle the cherry tomatoes on top and cook a little longer, for about 10 minutes, at low heat.

Remove on a plate and and shred the meat using two forks.

Mix with the basil paste and serve on lettuce leaves.

Sweet and sour chicken

Ingredients

- 1 chicken breast, cut into small cubes
- ½ yellow bell pepper, diced
- ½ red bell pepper, diced
- ½ green bell pepper, diced
- 1 spoon of lemon juice
- ¼ cup of raw honey
- 2 garlic cloves, chopped
- ½ teaspoon of freshly grated ginger
- 4 thin spring onions, chopped
- 1 teaspoon of sesame oil
- ¼ cup of water
- 2 spoons of coconut oil
- salt and pepper to taste

For the dough

- ½ teaspoon of Himalayan salt
- 1 teaspoon of ginger powder
- ½ teaspoon of garlic powder
- ½ teaspoon of onion powder
- ¼ cup of coconut flour
- 2 spoons of sesame seeds

Preparation

Mix all the ingredients for the dough in a bowl and stir to coat the chicken.

Place all the coated chicken pieces on a tray prepared with parchment paper for the preheated oven. Bake for 20 minutes, at medium heat (176°C or 350°F).

Meanwhile, prepare the sauce.

Sauté the bell peppers in a preheated pan until they become a bit soft.

Add the spring onions, garlic and ginger. Pour the water and honey and let them cook on low heat until the sauce starts to bubble and thicken a bit. Remove from the heat and add the lemon juice and the sesame oil.

Place the chicken pieces in the sauce and stir to coat. Serve with cauliflower rice.

Asian salmon with salad and asparagus

Ingredients

- 1 piece of fresh salmon (about 150 grams or 5.2 ounces)
- ½ teaspoon of freshly grated ginger
- ½ teaspoon of raw honey
- ½ teaspoon of naturally smoked paprika
- 1 spoon of sesame oil
- 1 garlic clove, chopped
- salt and pepper to taste

For the salad

- 2 cups of fresh valerian leaves
- 1 Fabio cucumber (or any long cucumber), spiralized
- 6 spears of asparagus
- 1 spoon of ghee
- ½ teaspoon of white sesame seeds (optional)
- ½ teaspoon of black sesame seeds (optional)
- 1 spoon of lemon juice
- salt and pepper to taste

Preparation

Put all the spices for the salmon in a bowl, mix well and season the salmon piece using your fingers. Let marinate for 15 minutes.

Wash and season the salad with salt, pepper, and lemon juice.

Heat up a frying pan and pour the ghee in it. Fry the salmon on both sides, at medium heat, until crusty. Leave a little bit on low heat, lid on, until fully cooked. Add the asparagus pieces on top, in the same pan and cook them in the released heat for a few minutes.

Place the salmon on the salad, in the bowl and sprinkle the sesame seeds on top. Serve immediately.

Traditional Romanian stewed cabbage

Ingredients

- 1 big white cabbage, sliced thin
- 750 grams (26 ounces) of pork, minced
- 1 big white onion, chopped
- 1 spoon of dry thyme leaves
- 1 spoon of dry dill leaves
- 2 and a half cups of tomato purée
- salt and pepper to taste
- 1 cup of still water
- 4 spoons of ghee or coconut oil

Preparation

Sauté the sliced cabbage in two spoons of coconut oil until it becomes soft. Season with thyme, salt, pepper, and dill leaves. Remove and set aside, in a dish.

Add the other 2 spoons of coconut oil to the pan and sauté the onion until it becomes translucent. Then add the minced meat and cook until it changes color. Season with salt, pepper, thyme, and dill leaves.

In an oven dish- preferably a clay pot if you have-start building a layer of cabbage and a layer of meat. When ready, pour the tomato purée and water on top and place the dish in the preheated oven.

Cook for about an hour, lid on, at medium heat (176°C or 350°F). Sprinkle some dill leaves on top when ready and serve.

Fish fingers with tartar sauce

Ingredients

- 600 grams (21 ounces) of Atlantic wild cod

For the dough

- 1 cup of almond flour
- 1 spoon of coconut flour
- ½ teaspoon of Himalayan salt
- ½ teaspoon of garlic powder
- coconut oil for frying

- juice from one lemon (optional)
- tartar sauce (recipe on page 124)

Preparation

Cut the fish into pieces to a preferred size. Season with salt and pepper to taste.

Put all the ingredients for the dough in a bowl and mix well with a whisk.

Coat every single piece of the cod and fry in coconut oil. Optionally you could bake them in the preheated oven for about 15 minutes, at medium heat (176°C or 350°F) but they will not be as crunchy.

Serve with tartar sauce and lemon juice sprinkled on top.

Crunchy crust trout fillet

Ingredients

- 600 grams of trout fillet
- salt and pepper to taste
- ½ spoon of lemon juice
- coconut oil for frying

For the crust:

- ½ teaspoon of garlic powder
- ½ cup of almond flour
- salt and pepper to taste

For the sauce:

- ¼ cup of mayonnaise (recipe on page 60)
- 2 garlic cloves, minced
- ¼ teaspoon of sea salt
- ½ teaspoon of lemon juice

Preparation

Season the fish with salt and pepper.

Place all ingredients for the crust in a dish and whisk well.

Coat the trout on all sides. Fry the trout fillet in coconut oil, in a preheated pan, at medium heat.

Mix the ingredients for the sauce in a small bowl and set aside.

Sprinkle lemon juice on top and serve.

Pork tenderloin with spinach and white sauce

Ingredients

- 500 grams of sliced pork tenderloin
- 1 white onion, chopped
- 2 garlic cloves, chopped
- 1 zucchini, cut into small cubes
- 2 cups of chopped spinach, fresh or frozen
- salt, pepper and paprika to season the meat
- 2 spoons of ghee or coconut oil
- 1 teaspoon of fresh parsley leaves, chopped

For the sauce

- ½ cup of Cajun nuts, soaked in hot water for 30 minutes
- 2 garlic cloves, minced
- ½ cup of coconut cream

Preparation

Season the meat with salt, pepper and paprika. Heat up a frying pan and sauté the onion and garlic at low heat, until the onion turns translucent.

Fry the meat in the same pan, until crusty. Add enough water to cover the meat and let it cook at low heat, lid on, for about 30 minutes. Then add the zucchini and spinach and cook together for a few more minutes, until the zucchini becomes soft.

Meanwhile, add all the sauce ingredients in the food processor and mix to a fine creamy texture.

Pour the sauce, wait to boil for another minute and remove from the heat. Leave the lid on for another 5 minutes to allow the flavors to combine.

Sprinkle the fresh parsley leaves on top and serve with the favorite vegetables or with mashed cauliflower.

One pot sausage and vegetables

Ingredients

- 10-11 pieces of pork sausage, cut at approximately 4 cm length
- 6 white champignon (white button) mushrooms, sliced
- 2 yellow bell peppers, diced
- 4 pieces of spring onions, chopped
- 1 cup of green beans, cut in smaller pieces
- 10 spears of asparagus, whole
- 1 spoon of ghee

Preparation

Sauté the pepper and mushrooms in a heated frying pan, with the spoon of ghee, at medium heat.

Add the sausage and then the onion. Cook together until you see a crust forming on the sides of the sausage. Add the green beans and asparagus and put the lid on.

Cook further at low heat, lid on, until ready, and serve.

Mini Pork Burgers with Coleslaw (10 mini burgers)

Ingredients

- 600 grams of minced pork
- 2 eggs
- 1 spoon of parsley leaves, chopped
- 3 garlic cloves, minced
- 2 green onions, chopped
- ½ cup of almond flour
- 20 pieces of big champignon (white button) mushrooms
- salt and pepper to taste
- coconut oil to fry

For the coleslaw

- 1 small white cabbage, sliced thin (approximately 4 cups)
- 2 grated carrots
- ½ cup of mayonnaise (recipe on page 123)
- salt and pepper to taste

Preparation

Place all the ingredients for the burgers in a bowl and mix well. Using your fingers, make the mini burger patties at the size of the mushrooms. Fry them one by one, in coconut oil, at medium heat and then remove them on a plate.

Wash the mushrooms and remove the stems. Fry them in a heated pan for a few minutes, at low heat, so they release a bit of water but their texture remains hard.

Mix and season all ingredients for the coleslaw in a separate dish.

Build the mini burgers using the mushrooms as buns and adding coleslaw on top and enjoy!

Note: These burgers freeze well so you can cook only as many as you need for a meal and freeze the rest.

Baked meatballs

Ingredients

- 2 white onions, chopped
- 5 garlic cloves, minced
- 1 kg (2.20 pounds) of minced veal
- 2 eggs
- 3 spoons of fresh parsley leaves, chopped
- 1 spoon of ghee to sauté the onions
- ½ cup of tomato purée
- 1 teaspoon of Himalayan salt
- 1 teaspoon of black pepper
- 1 teaspoon of paprika
- 1 teaspoon of garlic powder
- 1 teaspoon of ginger powder

Preparation

Sauté the onion in a frying pan, with the ghee, until it becomes translucent and softens. Set aside to cool.

Mix all the other ingredients in a dish and add the cooled onion. Use your hands to thoroughly mix everything into the ground meat.

Have an oven tray ready with the baking sheet on. Pinch off a piece of the meat mixture and gently roll between your hands to form 1 1/2-inch meatballs (about 2 tablespoons each). Continue shaping until all the meat is used, placing the meatballs on the baking sheet so that they are not touching.

Cook for 45 minutes in the preheated oven, at medium heat (176°C or 350°F).

Serve with favorite vegetables or with zucchini spaghetti and sauce.

Stuffed pork shoulder

Ingredients

- 1 kg (2.20 pounds) of pork shoulder
- 4-5 garlic cloves, halved
- 10 slices of naturally smoked bacon, cut into small pieces
- ½ teaspoon of dry thyme
- 2 spoons of melted ghee
- salt and pepper to taste
- ½ cup of water

Preparation

Make small incisions in the pork and stuff them with bacon and garlic cloves. Season with salt, pepper, and the thyme leaves. Place the meat in an oven. Pour the ghee over and add the cup of water.

Cook at medium heat, (176°C or 350°F), in the preheated oven, for about one hour and a half, with the lid on. Serve with favorite vegetables.

Mayonnaise

Ingredients

- 2 egg yolks
- ½ teaspoon of mustard powder
- 1 ½ tablespoon of lemon juice
- ½ teaspoon of salt
- ½ cup of olive oil

Preparation

Stir the egg yolks with mustard powder and mix in the food processor. Gradually add a litlle olive oil at a time so that the mayonnaise does not separate.

When thickened, you can add salt and lemon juice and then all the remaining olive oil while stirring constantly.

Store in a glass jar and keep in the refrigerator.

I like to do this by hand as well, but I add very little olive oil at a time, while stirring constantly with a wooden spoon.

Tartar sauce

Ingredients

- 4 tablespoons of mayonnaise
- 1 medium-sized pickled cucumber
- 2 tablespoons of pickled cucumber juice
- 1 teaspoon of lemon juice
- ¼ teaspoon of Himalayan salt
- 1 tablespoon of fresh dill, chopped

Preparation

Grate the pickled cucumber and then mix in a glass or porcelain bowl along with all the other ingredients.

Store in a jar in the refrigerator.

Cremwurst chicken

Ingredients

- 3 chicken breasts, no skin or bone (1600 grams), minced twice
- 2 teaspoons of Himalayan salt
- 1 teaspoon of black pepper
- 1/2 teaspoon of cumin powder
- 1 teaspoon of coriander powder
- 1 teaspoon of garlic powder
- 1/2 teaspoon of turmeric powder
- 1 egg
- 1 white onion, chopped
- 1/4 cup of ghee
- 1/4 cup of chicken broth
- 1 pack of sheep or pig casings

Preparation

Remove the casings from the pack and wash well in warm salt water. Then let them soak in water with a bit of apple cider vinegar.

Place all the other ingredients in a bowl and use your hands to thoroughly mix everything into the ground meat.

Prepare the sausage machine with the soaked casings. Form the cremwurst to your favorite size and cut off the casings enough to make a knot at each end.

Heat up a pot with water, a little salt, two bay leaves and some coriander seeds. Boil the cremwurst for 15-20 minutes until they harden and shrink.

Remove them and serve with any veggies you prefer. They make a great breakfast option as well.

Note: They freeze well. Just boil them in water for 2-3 minutes or heat them in a frying pan with a bit of ghee or coconut oil and they are ready to be served. If you want them more tender, leave the skin and fat on and mince with the meat.

You can also find the recipe on my blog, anourishedhome.com

Asparagus and mushroom cauliflower "rice"

Ingredients

- 1 medium size cauliflower, riced
- 1 white onion, diced
- 3 garlic cloves, sliced
- 1 spoon of fresh parsley leaves, chopped
- 3 big champignon mushrooms
- 10 asparagus spears, cut into small pieces
- 2 spoons of ghee, for cooking
- salt and pepper to taste

Preparation

Heat a frying pan and add the two spoons of ghee. Sauté the onion at medium heat until it becomes translucent.

Add the mushrooms and garlic. Let them cook at low heat and when almost ready add the riced cauliflower. Cover with a lid and cook for another 5 minutes, at low heat, until the "rice" starts to soften a bit. Stir a bit and place the asparagus in the pan.

Let them all cook on low heat for 3 more minutes, lid on, and then remove the pan from the heat.

Add the chopped parsley and mix well. Season with salt and pepper and serve immediately.

Vegetable lentils

Ingredients

- 1 small cauliflower or half the regular size cauliflower
- 5 small and thin carrots, whole
- 5 small and thin parsley roots, whole
- 3 spring onions, whole
- 3 small red beets, whole
- 2 cups of lentils, soaked in water for a minimum of 12 hours
- 1 white onion, chopped
- 2 cups of baby spinach, fresh
- 6 garlic cloves, whole
- 1 teaspoon of turmeric
- 1 teaspoon of rosemary leaves
- 2 spoons of ghee plus one more to cook
- salt and pepper to taste

Preparation

Wash the lentils well and let them soak in water for at least 12 hours. Throw the water repeatedly and add fresh clean water to the lentils. Once they have soaked for the minimum 12 hours wash again.

Wash and cut all the vegetables. Open the cauliflower in smaller florets and cut the carrots and parsley root in halves, length wise. Leave the onions and beets whole.

Place the cauliflower, carrots, parsley, green onions, beets and garlic in a big bowl and season with salt, pepper, and rosemary leaves. Pour the melted ghee on top and mix to coat them well.

Place the vegetables on a baking tray and bake in the preheated oven, at medium heat (176°C or 350°F) for 35-45 minutes. Check every 15 minutes and turn them over to ensure they do not burn. Depending on your oven, you may need less baking time.

Meanwhile sauté the onion in a frying pan, at medium heat, with a little ghee. When the onion changes color and becomes translucent, add the lentils and enough water to cover them. Season with salt and turmeric and cook at medium heat, for about 15-20 minutes, until ready. Add the spinach leaves, mix well, and remove from the heat.

Plate with baked vegetables as soon as they are all ready and enjoy!

Chanterelle mushrooms with pumpkin gnocchi

Ingredients

For the sauce

- 2 small white onions, chopped
- 4 garlic cloves, sliced
- 3 cups of chanterelle mushrooms, cut in big pieces or whole
- 2 cups of pumpkin gnocchi
- 1 spoon of ghee
- 5-6 sage leaves, fresh or dry
- salt and pepper to taste

For the gnocchi

- 1 cup pumpkin purée (store bought or freshly made)
- 3 eggs
- 1/2 teaspoon Himalayan salt
- 1 cup and a half of coconut flour

Preparation

Sauté the onion in a heated frying pan, at medium heat, until it becomes translucent. Add the mushrooms, garlic, and all the remaining ingredients.

Cook for 5-10 minutes, at low heat, with the lid on and then remove the lid until the excess water evaporates.

Mix all ingredients for the gnocchi in the food processor or in a bowl using a whisk. The texture of the dough should be that of wet sand, which can be easily shaped.

Give them a rectangular shape by hand or, if you have other preferences, the preferred shape. Poke them with a fork and make dentures to help them retain as much sauce as possible. Place them on a tray prepared with baking paper and bake in the preheated oven for about 10 minutes, at medium heat (176°C or 350°F).

Turn them on the other side and bake for another 5-10 minutes. Let them cool on a pastry grill.

Once cooled enough, add the fresh gnocchi to the mushrooms and serve immediately.

Vegetable casserole

Ingredients

- 1 zucchini, spiralized linguine
- 1 carrot, spiralized linguine
- 1 parsnip, spiralized linguine
- 2 cups of cauliflower, florets
- 2 cups of broccoli, florets
- 1 leek, chopped
- 1 red bell pepper, cut into small pieces
- 2 cups of champignon (white button) mushrooms, chopped
- 1 onion, chopped
- 4 garlic cloves, chopped
- 2 spoons of ghee, coconut oil or olive oil
- 1 spoon of green thyme leaves
- 1 spoon of green dill leaves
- salt and pepper to taste
- 1 teaspoon of turmeric
- ¼ cup of water

For the sauce:

- 1 cup of Cajun nuts, soaked for 30 minutes in hot water
- 1 cup of coconut cream
- 2 spoons of dried inactive yeast (optional, omit for the first 6 months on diet)
- 2 garlic cloves
- ¼ teaspoon of salt
- 1 spoon of lemon juice

Preparation

Sauté the leek, bell pepper and garlic in a preheated pan, at medium heat, until they soften.

Then add the mushrooms, cauliflower, and broccoli. Pour a ¼ cup of water in the pan and season with salt, pepper, and turmeric. Let them cook for about 10 more minutes, at low heat, with the lid on.

To make the sauce, add all the ingredients in the food processor and blend until creamy.

Remove the vegetables from the pan and place in a casserole. Sprinkle thyme and dill leaves and add the spiralized vegetables. Pour the sauce over everything and bake in the preheated oven at medium heat (176°C or 350°F) for 15 minutes and then serve.

Vegetable and bean humus bowl

Ingredients

- 1 and a half cups of white Navy beans, soaked in water for minimum 12 hours
- 1 cup of small broccoli florets
- 2 small and thin carrots
- 1 small and thin parsley root
- 4-5 cherry tomatoes, cut in halves or quarters
- 1 small red beet, sliced
- ½ cup of valerian leaves
- 1 small red onion, sliced
- 1 teaspoon of white sesame seeds (optional)
- 1 teaspoon of black sesame seeds (optional)
- 1 spoon of pumpkin seeds, soaked in water for minimum 8 hours
- 1 garlic clove, sliced
- ½ cup of zucchini, sliced
- 1 spoon of ghee
- salt and pepper to taste
- 2 spoons of olive oil
- 2 spoons of water

Preparation

Wash well the soaked beans and boil in salty water. When cooked, chill and place in the food processor with 2 spoons of olive oil and 2 spoons of water. Mix until it all becomes a smooth paste. If necessary, add a little bit more water.

Sauté the carrot and the parsley root with the spoon of ghee in a heated frying pan, at medium heat. Remove and place on a plate. Add to the pan a spoon of water and cook the broccoli with garlic, onion, and zucchini for 2-3 minutes, at medium heat, with the lid on.

Place everything in a bowl together with the raw ingredients and serve immediately.

Nutritious vegetable bowl

Ingredients (serves 2)

- 1 cup of white Navy beans, soaked in water for at least 12 hours
- 2-3 Bok Choi leaves, cut in small slices
- 1 cup of spinach and rucola or fresh mixed greens
- 1 fresh cucumber, sliced
- 1 cup of riced cauliflower
- 1 spoon of green parsley leaves, chopped
- 2 spoons of tahini (optional)
- 1 teaspoon of black sesame seeds (optional)
- 1 avocado, sliced
- 2 white button (champignon) mushrooms
- 2 brown button (champignon) mushrooms
- 1 oister mushroom
- 2 garlic cloves
- salt and pepper to taste
- 2 spoons of lemon juice
- 2 spoons of ghee, for cooking
- optional-a few slices of red-hot chilli pepper

Preparation

Boil the beans in salty water. Fry the mushrooms with the garlic in a heated frying pan, with the spoon of ghee, at medium heat, until they soften a little and change color. Add the Bok Choi leaves and sauté for a few minutes, at low heat.

Place half of all ingredients in two separate bowls. Season with salt and pepper to taste, pour the lemon juice and the tahini and sprinkle the sesame seeds on top. Serve fresh.

Boletus mushroom mini pizzas

Ingredients

- 1 big eggplant, cut in slices of 2 cm (about 0.8 inch) thick
- 2 cups of boletus mushrooms, fresh or frozen, chopped
- 1 spoon of fresh parsley leaves, chopped
- 1 spoon of ghee

For the sauce:

- 1 spoon of ghee
- 1 small white onion, chopped
- 2 garlic cloves, chopped
- 1 cup of tomato purée
- 1 teaspoon of fresh or dry basil leaves
- ½ teaspoon of dried oregano leaves
- 1 spoon of dry inactive yeast (optional, omit for the first 6 months on diet)
- salt and pepper to taste

Preparation

Wash the eggplant and cut it into 2 cm thick slices. Sprinkle with salt and pepper, rub a little ghee on all sides and cook in the preheated oven for 30 minutes, at medium heat (176°C or 350°F). Turn them over after the first 15 minutes and cook on the other side for the remaining 15.

Meawhile, prepare the sauce. Sauté the onion with the garlic in a heated frying pan, at medium heat, with the spoon of ghee. When the onion turns translucent, add the tomato purée, oregano, basil, salt, and pepper and cook at low to medium heat for about 10 minutes or until the sauce thickens enough.

In a differet pan fry the mushrooms with the spoon of ghee and cook with the lid on at medium heat until ready-around 10-15 minutes.

Place the slices of eggplant on a platter, top generously with the tomato sauce, add the mushrooms on top and sprinkle with the fresh parsley leaves.

Serve immediately.

Cauliflower rice with mushrooms and spinach

Ingredients

- 1 small cauliflower or half a regular size cauliflower, riced
- 1 white onion, chopped
- 2 garlic cloves, minced
- 2 cups of mixed forest mushrooms or any of your favorite mushrooms
- 1 spoon of ghee or coconut oil, for frying
- 3 cups of baby spinach, fresh
- salt and pepper to taste
- 1 teaspoon of turmeric

Preparation

Sauté the onion and garlic with the mushrooms in a frying pan, at medium heat, with the spoon of ghee.

Add the riced cauliflower and cook together for about 5 minutes, until the cauliflower softens but keeps the texture and consistency of boiled rice.

Add the spices and spinach and remove from the heat. Mix well and serve immediately.

Zucchini "spaghetti" with mixed mushrooms

Ingredients

- 2 cups of mixed wild mushrooms
- 1 white onion, chopped
- 2 garlic cloves, minced
- 1 zucchini, spiralized
- 1 spoon of ghee for cooking
- ½ spoon of fresh parsley leaves, chopped
- salt and pepper to taste

Preparation

Sauté the mushrooms, onion, and garlic with the spoon of ghee, at low heat, until fully cooked (about 15 minutes).

Add the spiralized zucchini and cook for a few more minutes, until the "spaghetti" soften slightly.

Season with salt and pepper and serve immediately.

Lentil soup with "rice" and kale

Ingredients

- 2 cups of red lentils soaked in water for a minimum of 12 hours
- ½ regular size cauliflower, riced
- 1 white onion, chopped
- 2 garlic cloves, minced
- 4-5 kale leaves, depending on size, chopped
- ½ cup of tomato purée
- ½ cup of coconut cream
- 1 spoon of ghee for cooking
- ½ spoon of turmeric
- 1 teaspoon of curry powder
- 1 spoon of fresh parsley leaves, chopped
- 3 spoons of dehydrated vegetables: parsley root, parsnip, celery root and carrot (optional)
- 1 teaspoon of dried marjoram leaves
- half a red-hot chilli pepper, sliced (optional)
- salt and pepper to taste

Preparation

In a hot frying pan pour the ghee and sauté the onion and garlic at low heat.

Add the lentils and cook for another 2-3 minutes, then add water to cover everything. Let them boil at medium heat.

After boiling for 10 minutes add the kale leaves, chopped and stems removed and all other ingredients, except for the coconut cream and fresh parsley leaves.

They should be completely cooked after another 15-20 minutes.

Remove from the heat and pour the coconut cream. Sprinkle the parsley leaves and mix well. Enjoy!

Pesto spaghetti

Ingredients

- 1 zucchini, spiralized

For the pesto

- 1 avocado
- ¼ cup of pine nuts, roasted
- 1 cup of fresh basil leaves
- 1 spoon of lemon juice
- 1 spoon of olive oil
- salt and pepper to taste

Preparation

Spiralize the zuchinni and cook it in a preheated oven at medium heat (176°C or 350°F) or in a preheated pan until the spaghetti soften-for around 2-3 minutes.

Roast the pine nuts in a frying pan at medium heat, for a few minutes and place them in the food processor with the remaining pesto ingredients. Blend until you get a fine creamy sauce.

Mix with the zucchini pasta and serve.

Nutritious bowl with pumpkin and vegetables

Ingredients

- 1 cup and a half of pumpkin purée (store bought or freshly made)
- 1 spoon of melted ghee
- ½ a red bell pepper, baked and sliced
- 4-5 slices of zucchini, grilled
- 1 parsley root, baked
- 1 cup of boletus mushrooms, diced
- 1 spoon of coconut oil or ghee
- 1 garlic clove, minced
- salt and pepper to taste

Preparation

Mix the pumpkin purée with the spoon of ghee and salt to taste.

Wash, peel and cut the vegetables to grill or bake. You can place them on a tray and bake in the preheated oven, at medium heat (176°C or 350°F) for about 20 minutes or you could cook them in a preheated frying pan, at medium heat, until they change a bit the color and texture but remain firm.

Fry the boletus mushrooms in a pan with ghee and garlic, at medium heat, for about 10-15 minutes until they soften and shrink.

To make the pumpkin purée all you need is a small pumpkin or a few slices of it, washed and seeds removed.

Brush a little bit of ghee and sprinkle some salt on top and place them on a tray lined with parchment paper. Bake in the preheated oven, at about 200°C or 400°F for 45-60 minutes.

Allow the pumpkin to cool, scoop out the soft flesh into a food processor and blend at high speed until very smooth, 2-4 minutes.

Pour the pumpkin purée in a bowl and add everything else. Serve immediately.

Cauliflower with mushrooms and black lentils

Ingredients

- ½ cauliflower, cut into small florets
- 10 brown champignon (white button) mushrooms
- 7 garlic cloves, whole
- 2 spoons of ghee, melted
- 1 onion
- 1 cup of black lentils, soaked in water for minimum 12 hours and then boiled
- 1 teaspoon of thyme
- salt and pepper to taste

Preparation

Wash and cut the cauliflower in small florets, peel the garlic, and leave the cloves whole.

Clean the onion and cut into big chuncks. Mix the cauliflower, onion and garlic in a bowl and season with salt and pepper to taste. Add the dried thyme and the spoon of ghee.

Preheat the oven to 176°C or 350°F and line a baking sheet with parchment paper and bake them for 15-20 minutes.

Sauté the mushrooms separately with ghee, in a frying pan at medium heat, until they soften and shrink a bit.

When everything is cooked, mix with the lentils, and serve.

Eggplant roll with black lentil pâté

Ingredients

- 1 eggplant, cut thin slices, lengthwise

For the pâté

- 2 cups of black lentils, soaked in water for minimum 12 hours
- 1 white onion, chopped
- 1 garlic clove, chopped
- 1 spoon of ghee
- ½ teaspoon of fresh parsley leaves, chopped
- salt and pepper to taste

Preparation

Wash and cut the vegetables.

Leave the lentils to soak for at least 12 hours, wash well, change the water and boil them with a little salt.

Slice the eggplant in thin slices of about 1 cm, lengthwise, and season with salt and pepper.

Bake in the preheated oven, at medium heat (176°C or 350°F) for about 10 minutes, until tender.

Sauté the onion and garlic with the spoon of ghee, in a frying pan, at medium heat. Add the lentils and parsley leaves and mix well. Optionally, you could add 2 spoons of dry inactive yeast (omit in the first 6 months of diet).

Place the eggplant slices on a plate, spoon some lentil pâté on the slices and roll slowly. Serve fresh.

Pumpkin with root vegetables and bacon

Ingredients

- 1 small butternut pumpkin
- 1 small celery root
- 2 medium size carrots
- 1 small parsnip
- 1 teaspoon of dried thyme leaves
- 1 teaspoon of dried rosemary leaves
- 1 spoon of ghee or coconut oil
- 10 bacon slices
- salt and pepper to taste

Preparation

Wash, peel and cut the vegetables in small cubes. Add them all in a bowl with the remaining ingredients, except for bacon, and mix well. Bake in the preheated oven, at medium heat (176°C or 350°F) for about 25-30 minutes.

If you prefer, you could bake the pumpkin separately, skin on, but it will take longer to cook. You would need to wash and cut the pumpkin in half. Brush a little bit of ghee and sprinkle some salt on top and place the halves on a tray lined with parchment paper. Bake in the preheated oven, at about 200°C or 400°F for 45-60 minutes.

Once it cools enough to cut, scoop it out and dice it.

Fry the bacon slices in a frying pan, at medium heat, until crispy. Let them cool on a plate.

When the vegetables are ready, place them and the pumpkin in a serving bowl. Sprinkle the bacon on top and serve immediately.

Vegetable patties with white sauce

Ingredients

For the patties

- 1 medium size carrot, grated
- 1 celery root, grated
- 1 small courgette, grated and squeezed
- 1 white onion, chopped small
- 3 garlic cloves, minced
- ½ spoon of fresh dill leaves, chopped
- ½ spoon of fresh parsley leaves, chopped
- 1 spoon of ghee or coconut oil for cooking
- ½ cup of almond flour
- 2 eggs

For the sauce

- ½ cup of Cajun nuts, soaked in hot water for 30 minutes
- ¼ cup of coconut cream
- ¼ cup of still water plus 2 more spoons
- 1 spoon and a half of lemon juice
- 1 spoon of olive oil
- 2 spoons of chives, finely chopped

Preparation

Cook all the ingredients in a heated pan, with the two spoons of ghee or coconut oil until the onion softens and the courgette releases the remaining water. Let them cool in a sieve and squeeze the excess water. Place in a bowl with the remaining ingredients.

Form the vegetable patties with your fingers and cook in the preheated oven at medium heat (176°C or 350°F) for 15-20 minutes.

While they cook, make the sauce. Except for the chopped chives, add all sauce ingredients in the food processor and blend them to a cream consistency. Add the chopped chives and mix with a spoon.

Remove the vegetable patties from the oven and serve fresh with the dipping sauce.

Note: The patties freeze well so I usually make a few batches at a time. Simply remove them from the freezer and leave them in the fridge overnight to defreeze slowly. Heat them up in the oven or in a frying pan, at low heat.

Vegetable zucchini noodles

Ingredients

- 1 zucchini, fresh, spiralized in fine noodles
- 4 champignon (white button) mushrooms, sliced
- 1 green bell pepper, cut julienne
- 1 carrot, cut julienne
- 2 garlic cloves, minced
- 1 cup of pea pods
- 2 spoons of coconut oil
- salt and pepper to taste
- 1 spoon of sesame oil
- 1 teaspoon of lemon juice
- ½ teaspoon of black sesame seeds (optional)

Preparation

Sauté the mushrooms with the garlic and the two spoons of coconut oil in a heated frying pan, at medium heat for about 5 minutes. Then add the carrot and the peppers and cook together until they soften but remain crunchy at the same time, approximately 5-10 minutes, at medium heat.

Add the zucchini noodles to the pan and mix well. Remove from the heat. Pour the sesame oil, lemon juice and sprinkle the sesame seeds on top.

Serve immediately.

Slow roasted Romanian cabbage with bacon

Ingredients

- 1 white cabbage, medium size
- 6-7 bacon slices, cut into small pieces
- 2 spoons of ghee or coconut oil
- 1 spoon of dried thyme
- ½ spoon of dried dill leaves
- ½ cup of tomato purée
- salt and pepper to taste

Preparation

Cut the cabbage into thin slices and season to taste with salt and pepper.

Cook the bacon in a heated frying pan, until it leaves the fat and roasts a little. Add the two spoons of ghee and cabbage to the pan and roast under low heat, lid on, until it softens and changes the texture.

Add the tomato purée, thyme and dill and let it cook slowly for another 35-45 minutes, at low heat, lid on.

The cabbage will be soft and full of flavor.

Stuffed Pattypan Squash

Ingredients

- 1 Pattypan Squash or else another favorite kind of Squash
- 1 red bell pepper, sliced small
- 1 white onion, chopped
- 2 garlic cloves, chopped
- 1 kale leaf, stem removed and chopped
- 1 spoon of coconut oil
- ½ cup of champignon mushrooms, sliced
- salt and pepper to taste

For the stuffing

- ½ cup of Cajun nuts, soaked in hot water for 30 minutes
- 1 spoon of fresh parsley leaves
- 1 spoon of fresh dill leaves
- 1 teaspoon of apple cider vinegar

Preparation

Wash the squash, slice off its top and scoop out all the seeds with a spoon. Use a pastry brush to paint a layer of ghee inside the squash and sprinkle salt and pepper to taste.

Sauté the onion and bell pepper with the coconut oil in a preheated pan, at medium heat. Add the garlic, the kale, and mushrooms to the pan. Cook until the vegetables change color and soften, about 10 minutes, at medium heat. Season with salt and pepper to taste.

Put all the ingredients for the sauce in the food processor and mix with a pinch of salt until you get a creamy sauce, with the consistency of a think sour cream. If you need to, add some patter to reach this texture.

Mix the sauce with the vegetables and stuff the squah. Place the sliced top back on and bake in the oven at low heat (65°C or 150°F) for an hour.

Serve immediately.

Stuffed eggplant

Ingredients

- 1 eggplant
- 1 white onion, chopped
- 2 garlic cloves, chopped
- ½ cup of minced pork
- ½ teaspoon of paprika
- salt and pepper to taste
- 1 spoon of ghee or olive oil
- ½ spoon of fresh parsley leaves, chopped
- ¼ cup of purée tomatoes

Preparation

Wash the eggplant and cut in half, lengthwise. Season with salt, pepper and paprika and paint a thin layer of ghee or olive oil on top.

Bake in the preheated oven, at medium heat, (176°C or 350°F) for about 35 minutes. When is cooked, you will notice that the center is soft and easy to scoop out, but the skin is still strong enough to hold its shape. Be careful not to overcook it-it will soften too much.

Sauté the onion in a frying pan, at medium heat, with the coconut oil until becomes translucent. Add the meat and cook fully, lid on.

Scoop the center of the eggplant, leaving enough meat inside the skin that can hold its shape. Add the scooped pieces to the dish with the cooked meat and onions and let them simmer for another minute or two so the flavours blend.

Remove from the heat add the parsley leaves and season with salt and pepper to taste.

Stuff the eggplant with all this goodness and serve immediately.

Cauliflower purée with baked vegetables

Ingredients

- ½ yellow bell pepper
- ½ red bell pepper
- ½ zucchini
- 1 white onion, sliced
- 3 champignon (white button) mushrooms, sliced
- ½ carrot, sliced
- olive oil for greasing the vegetables
- salt and pepper to taste

For the purée

- 1 small cauliflower, boiled in salty water
- 1 spoon of olive oil
- salt and pepper to taste

Preparation

Place all the vegetables in a bowl, season with salt and pepper and grease with olive oil. Bake them in the preheated oven for about 20-25 minutes at medium heat (176°C or 350°F). Turn them over every 10 minutes so they bake evenly and do not burn.

Meanwhile, add all the ingredients for the purée in the food processor and mix until you get a fine texture.

Place the purée in a serving bowl, add all the vegetables on top and enjoy.

Ratatouille

Ingredients

- 1 white onion, chopped big chuncks
- 1 yellow bell pepper, chopped big chuncks
- 1 courgette, chopped big chunks
- 1 eggplant, chopped big chunks
- 3 tomatoes, diced
- 2 garlic cloves, chopped
- 3 spoons of olive oil
- 1 cup of tomato purée
- 1 spoon of fresh parsley leaves, broken by hand in bigger pieces
- 1 teaspoon of dry thyme
- salt and pepper to taste

Preparation

Heat a frying pan and pour the olive oil in it. Sauté the vegetables together until they change color and texture and then add the thyme and the tomato purée. Let them cook, lid on, until the sauce starts to thicken, about 30 minutes.

Season with salt and pepper, sprinkle the fresh parsley leaves on top and serve immediately.

Alfredo sauce tagliatelle

Ingredients

- 1 cup of chicken pieces-lunch leftovers or pieces of rotisserie chicken (about a full thigh)
- 1 fresh zucchini, spiralized tagliatelle
- 1 spoon of olive oil
- salt and pepper to taste

For the sauce

- ½ cup of Cajun nuts, soaked in hot water for 30 minutes
- 2 garlic cloves
- ½ cup of coconut cream
- 1 spoon of dry inactive yeast (optional-omit if on the first 6 months of diet)
- 1 spoon of still water (optional-you may need it to for texture)

Preparation

Place the sauce ingredients in the food processor and mix to get a fine texture, like the one of sour cream.

Cook the tagliatellele in a heated frying pan, at medium heat, with the olive oil, for about 1 minute, just enough to soften them.

Remove from the heat, add the chicken pieces and the sauce, and mix in the pan. Season with salt and pepper and serve immediately.

"Shepherd's" pie

Ingredients

- 1 cup of small cauliflower florets
- 1 cup of sliced champignon (white button) mushrooms
- ½ cup of small zucchini pieces
- ½ yellow bell pepper, small slices
- 1 small carrot, sliced
- 1 white onion, chopped
- 1 spring onion, finely chopped
- 1 spoon of olive oil, for sauté

For the sauce

- ½ cup of Cajun nuts, soaked in hot water for 30 minutes
- 2 garlic cloves
- ½ cup of coconut cream
- 1 spoon of dry inactive yeast (optional-omit if you are in the first 6 months of diet)
- 1 spoon of still water (optional-you may need it for texture)

For the dough

- 1 cup of almond flour
- 1 spoon of coconut flour
- 1 spoon of onion flakes
- ½ teaspoon of Himalayan salt
- 1 egg
- ¼ cup of melted ghee

Preparation

Sauté the vegetables in a heated frying pan, with the olive oil, at medium heat, until they change texture and color and become soft-about 10-15 minutes. Set aside.

Place all dry ingredients for the dough in the food processor and pulse a few times. Add the remaining ingredients for the dough and mix well, until the dough forms like a ball. Place on a piece of parchment paper and mold it with your fingers in a rectangle shape. Let it cool in the frigde for about 10 minutes.

Meanwhile, prepare the sauce.

Place all the ingredients for the sauce in the food processor and mix to a fine texture. Pour over the vegetables and incorporate.

Place them all in an oven dish prepared for baking, greased with a bit of ghee, of 20 cm length, 14 cm width and 5 cm height (7.8x5.5x1.9 inches).

Remove the dough from the fridge and roll it between two sheets of baking paper.

Place the dough it over the dish you already prepared with the vegetables for baking. Mold around the edges with your fingers and punch some holes on top with a fork.

Bake in the preheated oven, at medium heat (176°C or 350°F), for 10 minutes.

Serve immediately or the next day.

Note: This dough freezes well. You can prepare it ahead of time and freeze or keep in the fridge for those evenings when you do not find the time to do everything. ☺

Bean humus with caramelized onions and pine nuts

Ingredients

- 1 cup and a half of white beans, soaked for minimum 12 hours in water, water changed repeatedly
- 2 white onions, sliced Julienne
- 2 spoons of olive oil
- ½ spoon of pine nuts
- salt and pepper to taste

Preparation

Boil the soaked beans in water with salt. When cooked, set aside to cool, and then blend well to a fine paste. Add a bit of water or a little olive oil if needed.

Heat up a frying pan and cook the onion with a spoon of olive oil. To caramelize it, mix constantly at low heat, lid on. Cook slowly until it changes color and texture, and it becomes soft and brown.

Place the bean humus in a bowl, pour a spoon of olive oil on top, add the caramelized onion and the pine nuts. For more flavor, toast the pine nuts in a pan.

Eggplant dip with focaccia

Ingredients

- 2 eggplants, baked whole in the oven
- 1 white onion, medium size, chopped
- 2 spoons of olive oil
- ½ spoon of lemon juice
- 3 spoons of mayonnaise
- salt and pepper to taste

Preparation

Wash the eggplants and bake them whole, in the preheated oven, for about one hour at medium heat (176°C or 350°F). Turn them over after 30 minutes to ensure they bake evenly. When ready, remove the skin and let them cool a bit. Place them in the food processor and mix until you get a fine paste.

You can serve with focaccia or your own favorite bread.

You find the focaccia recipe below and in the bread recipe section of the book.

Ingredients for the focaccia:

- 1 cup of coconut flour
- ½ teaspoon of baking soda
- 4 eggs
- ½ cup of coconut cream
- ¼ cup of ghee
- ½ teaspoon of Himalaya salt
- ¼ teaspoon of white pepper
- 1 teaspoon of garlic powder
- 2 spoons of onion flakes
- ½ teaspoon of rosemary leaves, fresh
- 1 spoon of oregano leaves, fresh
- 1 spoon of thyme leaves, fresh

To prepare the focaccia, first chop all the green leaves with a knife.

Then place all the ingredients in the food processor and mix to make the dough. Pour the dough in an oven dish and bake at medium heat (176°C or 350°F) for about 20-25 minutes.

Thin crust pizza

Ingredients

For the tomato sauce

- 1 white onion, chopped
- 2 garlic cloves, chopped
- ¼ cup of fresh basil, largely chopped
- 1 cup of tomato purée
- salt and pepper to taste

For the dough

- 1 cup of almond flour
- 2 spoons of coconut flour
- ¼ teaspoon of Himalayan salt
- 2 eggs
- 1 spoon of ghee

For the topping

- 1 cup of fresh baby spinach
- 3 champignon (white button) mushrooms, sliced
- 5-6 black olives, sliced
- 3 cherry tomatoes, sliced

Preparation

Place all the ingredients for the dough in the food processor and mix well. Spread the dough between two baking sheets and stretch to a thickness of about 1 cm, giving a round shape.

To make the tomato sauce place all the ingredients in the food processor and mix to a creamy consistency. Boil it in a pan, at medium heat, until the sauce thickens, about 5-10 minutes.

Pour the sauce over the dough and spread it evenly on the entire surface. Place all the ingredients left on top and bake in the preheated oven, at medium heat (176°C or 350°F) for about 10 minutes.

Slice and serve immediately.

Thick crust pizza

Ingredients

For the dough

- 1 cup of almond flour
- ½ cup of coconut flour
- ½ cup of ghee
- ½ teaspoon of Himalayan salt
- 1 teaspoon of garlic powder
- ½ teaspoon of baking soda
- 2 eggs

For the sauce

- 4 garlic cloves
- 1 white onion, chopped
- 1 cup of freshly minced pork (optional)
- 2 cups of champignon (white button) mushrooms, finely chopped
- 2 cups of tomato purée
- 2 spoons of ghee (to sauté)
- ½ teaspoon of dried thyme leaves
- ½ teaspoon of parsley leaves
- salt and pepper to taste

Preparation

Place all the dry ingredients for the dough in the food processor and pulse a few times. Add the eggs and mix until everything is well incorporated. Prepare a square baking dish with the size of about 24 cm (9.44 inches) for the oven and line it with parchment paper.

In a heated frying pan, sauté the onion until it becomes translucent. Add the mushrooms, then the meat and the garlic. Pour the tomato purée, sprinkle the thyme leaves and season with salt and pepper. Cook the sauce until it thickens. When ready, add the fresh parsley leaves.

Place the dough in the dish and spoon it all out. Bake in the preheated oven for 5 minutes, at medium heat (176°C or 350°F). Then pour the sauce over it and cook for another 20 minutes, same temperature.

Let it cool. Slice and serve once it is cool enough.

Mini Pattypan squash with eggplant and aromatic herbs

Ingredients

- 10-12 garlic cloves, whole
- 6 mini Pattypan squash, about 8 cm diameter small, cut in halves, leghtwise (you can use any other type of squash or zucchini, cut in big pieces)
- 1 eggplant, cut in big pieces
- 1 teaspoon of dry thyme
- 1 teaspoon of rosemary leaves, dry or fresh
- 2 spoons of ghee, melted
- ½ teaspoon of garlic powder
- salt and pepper to taste

Preparation

Prepare a big baking tray and line it with parchment paper.

Place the vegetables and garlic on the tray, season with salt, pepper, garlic powder and aromatic herbs. Pour the melted ghee all over them. Mix well using your fingers so that you incoroporate all flavours.

Bake in the preheated oven, at medium heat, (176°C or 350°F) for about 45 minutes. During this time turn them over repeatedly so they bake on all sides.

Serve as soon as they are ready with your favorite meat dish or on their own.

English muffins

Ingredients

- 2 spoons of Cajun butter
- 2 spoons of coconut flour
- ½ teaspoons of aluminum-free baking soda
- ¼ Himalayan salt
- 1 teaspoon of almond flour
- 2 eggs

Preparation

Whisk all the ingredients in a bowl or mix them in the food processor. Grease two 9.5 cm (3.7 inches) diameter ramekins with coconut oil.

Split the dough in two equal amounts in the two ramekins. Bake in the preheated oven for 15 minutes at medium heat (176°C or 350°F).

Cool on a cooling rack. Serve cut in half for breakfast or else as burger buns.

Note: They freeze well, and they toast so nicely in a pan or in the toaster. Just make sure when you toast them that you don't use a toaster for regular bread, so you do not contaminate with gluten. You should have a separate toaster just for the grain free bread.

Sandwich bread

Ingredients

- 1 cup of almond flour
- ¼ almond butter
- ½ teaspoon of Himalayan salt
- ½ teaspoon of aluminum-free baking soda
- ½ cup of melted ghee
- 2 eggs
- 2 egg whites
- 1 teaspoon of apple cider vinegar

Preparation

Except for the egg whites, add all the other ingredients in the food processor and mix well. Beat the egg whites separately and incorporate carefully in the dough, without mixing too long.

Pour in a smaller size baking tray. I use a tray with the 25 cm length and 11 cm width (9.8x4.3 inches).

Bake in the preheated oven for 25 minutes, at medium heat (176°C or 350°F).

Slice after it cools.

Note: This bread freezes well. You can slice it, make a two-slice portion, and freeze this way, in separate bags.

Seeded bagels

Ingredients

- 1/3 cup of coconut flour
- ½ teaspoon of aluminum-free baking soda
- 4 eggs
- ½ teaspoon of Himalayan salt
- 1/3 cup of ghee
- 2 spoons of Cajun butter
- 1 teaspoon of apple cider vinegar
- 1 teaspoon of poppy seeds (optional)
- ½ teaspoon of black sesame seeds (optional)
- 1 teaspoon of white sesame seeds (optional)

Preparation

Except for the seeds, add all the ingredients in the food processor and mix or in a bowl and whisk well. The dough is going be soft and runny, kind of like the pancake dough.

Pour in the bagel mold and sprinkle the seeds on top.

Bake in the preheated oven for about 20 minutes, at medium heat (176°C or 350°F).

Out of this recipe you make 5 bagels with a 7 cm diameter (2.7 inches).

Artisan bread

Ingredients

- 2 cups of almond flour
- ½ teaspoon of aluminum-free baking soda
- ½ teaspoon of Himalayan salt
- 3 eggs-yolks separated
- ¼ cup of Cajun butter
- ½ cup of melted coconut oil
- ¼ cup of still water
- ¼ cup of coconut flour-split in half

Preparation

Except for the egg whites and the coconut flour, place all the ingredients in the food processor and mix well until you get the dough. Spoon the dough in a bowl.

Beat the egg whites separately and then incorporate them slowly in the dough with a whisk.

The dough will be soft. Sprinkle a little bit from half the amount of coconut flour over the dough and using the fingers from one hand knead slowly, as if you would work with a regular wheat bread. Knead slowly, lifting the dough up with the four fingers. Sprinkle a little bit more coconut flour and repeat. These movements absorb the excess of humidity and increase the dough viscosity.

Prepare a baking tray with baking paper. Sprinkle a little bit of coconut flour on top.

Split the dough into two and with the wet fingers shape two separate balls. Blow the excess of coconut flour off the tray because otherwise it will burn during baking.

Optionally, cut a cross with a knife in the middle of the dough balls. This way it will open during baking and will give the artisanal aspect.

Bake the bread in the preheated oven, at medium heat, (176°C or 350°F) for 35 minutes. Let it cool on a cooling rack and remove the excess coconut flour on top with the fingers.

Slice once it is cooled.

Note: This bread is full of flavor the following day.

Onion biscuits

Ingredients

- ½ cup of coconut flour
- 3 eggs
- ½ teaspoon of aluminum-free baking soda
- 1/3 cup of melted ghee
- 1 and a half spoon of onion flakes
- 1 spoon of chopped chives
- ½ teaspoon of garlic powder
- 1 teaspoon of apple cider vinegar

Preparation

Place all ingredients in a bowl and whisk well. Let the dough rest for 10 minutes.

Scoop the dough with an ice-cream spoon on a baking tray lined with parchment paper. Leave a little bit of distance between the dough balls since they will rise while cooking.

Bake in the preheated oven at medium heat (176°C or 350°F), for about 20 minutes.

Serve with breakfast or simply on their own, with a thin layer of ghee on top.

Note: These biscuits freeze well so I always make a few batches for those mornings when I am rushed to my day.

Aromatic herbs focaccia

Ingredients

- 1 cup of coconut flour
- ½ teaspoon of baking soda
- 4 eggs
- ½ cup of coconut cream
- ¼ cup of ghee
- ½ teaspoon of Himalaya salt
- ¼ teaspoon of white pepper
- 1 teaspoon of garlic powder
- 2 spoons of onion flakes
- ½ teaspoon of rosemary leaves, fresh
- 1 spoon of oregano leaves, fresh
- 1 spoon of thyme leaves, fresh

Preparation

Finely chop all the green leaves with a knife.

Then place all ingredients in the food processor and make the dough. The dough will be soft, so do not worry about the texture.

Pour the dough in an oven dish and bake at medium heat (176°C or 350°F) for 20-25 minutes.

Enjoy it with your favorite dishes.

Anti-inflammatory seeded bread

Ingredients

- 3 cups of almond flour
- 2 spoons of coconut flour
- ½ teaspoon of Himalayan salt
- 2 spoons of onion flakes
- ¼ teaspoon of black pepper
- ½ teaspoon of organic turmeric
- ½ teaspoon of aluminum-free baking soda
- 6 eggs
- 1 spoon of raw honey
- 1 spoon of sunflower seeds
- 1 spoon of pumpkin seeds
- 1 spoon of white sesame seeds (optional)
- 1 teaspoon of black sesame seeds (optional)

Preparation

Except for the seeds, place all the ingredients in the food processor and mix to make the dough.

Line the bottom of an 8.5×4.5-inch loaf pan with parchment paper. Pour the dough in and sprinkle the seeds on top.

Bake in the preheated oven for about 30 minutes at medium heat (176°C or 350°F).

Turkish pita bread

Ingredients

- 1 cup of almond flour
- 1/3 cup of coconut flour
- ¼ teaspoon of Himalayan salt
- ½ teaspoon of aluminum-free baking soda
- 2 eggs
- ¼ cup of ghee
- ½ teaspoon of cumin powder
- ¼ cup of coconut cream

Preparation

Add all the ingredients in the food processor and mix well until you get the dough.

Split into 4 equal parts and make 4 separate balls with the wet fingers. Place them at equal distance on a big baking tray, lined with parchment paper.

Flatten with wet palms to get 4 round flat breads of about a 1 cm (0.4 inches) thickness.

Bake at medium heat (176°C or 350°F) for 10 minutes and then turn off the heat and let them sit on the tray, in the oven, for another 3 minutes.

Serve with your favorite dish or cut in half with a small bread knife and stuff them with your favorite meats or vegetables.

They are great with chicken fajitas or cauliflower couscous.

Vegan dehydrated bread

Ingredients

- 1 cup of almond flour
- 1 red bell pepper
- 5 slices of sundried tomatoes
- 1 spoon of onion flakes
- ½ spoon of garlic flakes
- ½ teaspoon of Himalayan salt
- ¼ teaspoon of dried oregano leaves
- ¼ cup of sunflower seeds
- 1 spoon of ground sesame seeds (optional)

Preparation

Except for the seeds, place all ingredients in the food processor and mix until you get a homogenous paste.

Stretch between two sheets of parchment paper to a thickness of about 1 cm (0.4 inches).

Sprinkle the seeds on top and press carefully with the palms until they are all well incorporated.

Cut all slices with a pizza knife and bake in the oven at low heat (65°C or 150°F) for 20 minutes. Move the slices in the dehydrator and leave at 55 degrees Celsius (131 °F) for another hour.

If you do not have a dehydrator, continue to cook in the oven at lowest heat for about 40 minutes, checking constantly that they do not burn.

Crunchy salty crackers

Ingredients

- 1 egg
- 1 spoon of melted ghee
- 1 cup and a half of almond flour
- 1 spoon of black sesame seeds (optional)
- ½ teaspoon of Himalayan salt
- 1 teaspoon of dried oregano leaves
- 1 teaspoon of garlic powder

Preparation

Place all the dry ingredients in the food processor and pulse a few times. Add the egg and the ghee and mix well.

Remove the dough from the food processor and stretch it in between two sheets of parchment paper to a thickness of 1 cm (0.4 inches).

Cut to favorite shape with a pizza knife and bake in the preheated oven at medium heat (176°C or 350°F) for about 10 minutes.

Store the crackers in a tightly sealed container to keep their crunchy texture.

Custard and blueberry tart

Ingredients

For the crust

- 1 cup and a ¼ cup of almond flour
- 2 spoons of coconut flour
- 1 spoon of raw honey
- 1 egg
- ¼ cup of coconut oil

For the custard

- 8 yolks at room temperature
- 1 spoon of lemon zest
- 2 cups of coconut cream
- 2 spoons of raw honey
- 1 teaspoon of lemon juice
- 2 cups of fresh blueberries

Preparation

Place all the ingredients for the crust in the food processor and mix well. The dough needs to be dense, like a soft ball. Grease a tart dish with a little coconut oil and shape the crust in it, using your fingers. Punch holes with a fork in it and bake in the preheated oven for 10 minutes, at medium heat (176°C or 350°F).

Remove from the oven and let it cool.

Meanwhile, prepare a pot with boiling water and a glass container to place inside for bain-marie (double boiling). Use a heat-resistant glass container and be careful that the hot water does not touch its bottom.

Place all the custard ingredients inside the glass container, except for the lemon juice and mix with a whisk.

Cook slowly at low heat for about 20-25 minutes, mixing constantly. Cook until you see it thickens enough.

Remove from the heat and mix in the lemon juice. Let it cool until it doesn't burn but don't wait too long, so it does not harden too much. Around 10-15 minutes.

Once cooled, pour the entire custard inside the pie crust. Add the blueberries on top and transfer to the fridge until completely cold.

Note: This tart is more delicious the following day.

Raspberry Thumbprint Cookies

Ingredients

- 1 cup of almond flour
- ¼ cup of almond butter
- 2 spoons of coconut flour
- 2 spoons of melted ghee
- 2 spoons of raw honey
- 1/3 cup of fresh raspberries-around 12 pieces

Preparation

Place the flours, almond butter, ghee, and honey in the food processor and mix well. Shape the dough into small balls and press with the thumb to make a print in the middle.

Add a raspberry in each center.

Bake for 5-7 minutes in the preheated oven, at medium heat (176°C or 350°F).

Walnut Rugelach

Ingredients (14 pieces)

For the dough

- 1 and a half cups of almond flour
- 1 spoon of coconut flour
- 2 spoons of almond butter
- 1 egg
- 2 spoons of raw honey

For the stuffing

- 1 and a half cups of ground walnuts
- ¼ cup of raw honey
- ½ teaspoon of cinnamon powder
- ¼ teaspoon of freshly grated nutmeg

Preparation

Place all the ingredients for the dough in the food processor and mix well. Give the dough a square shape on a piece of parchment paper and leave it in the fridge for 30 minutes.

Meanwhile, place all the ingredients for stuffing in a pan at low heat. Mix constantly with a spatula to ensure they toast a little without burning. Remove the stuffing from the heat and set aside to cool.

Stretch the dough between two sheets of parchment paper and cut it into rectangle shapes, with the sides of about 6 and 8 cm (2.3 to 3 inches).

Use a teaspoon to place the stuffing in the middle and bring together the opposite sides, leaving the other two sides open.

Bake in the preheated oven for 10 minutes, at medium heat (176°C or 350°F).

Note: They freeze well. To defrost leave them in the fridge overnight and then place in the preheated oven, at medium heat, for about 3 minutes.

Red velvet cookies with cranberries and macadamia nuts

Ingredients

- 2 spoons of almond butter
- 1 cup of almond flour
- 2 spoons of red beet powder
- 1 egg
- 2 spoons of coconut oil
- 1 spoon of coconut flour
- 3 spoons of raw honey
- ¼ cup of dry cranberries
- ¼ cup of macadamia nuts

Preparation

Mix all the ingredients in a bowl. Take a little bit of dough at a time and roll into balls. Place them on the baking tray and flatten with the fingers.

Bake in the preheated oven, for 10 minutes at medium heat (176°C or 350°F).

Remove immediately and let them cool on a cooling rack.

Out of this dough you will make 8-9 cookies with a diameter of 5-6 cm (about 2.3 inches).

Forest fruit cake

Ingredients

The ingredients below are for one single layer of the cake. Double for the two-layer cake or bake the batter one by one if you only have one small baking dish.

- 1 cup of almond flour
- ¼ cup of coconut flour
- ½ teaspoon of aluminum-free baking soda
- 2 eggs

- ¼ cup of ghee
- ¼ cup of Madagascar vanilla powder
- ¼ cup of raw honey
- 1 teaspoon of lemon zest

For the vanilla cream
- 10 yolks
- 1 spoon of lemon zest
- 1 teaspoon of lemon juice

- 3 spoons of raw honey
- 2 cups of coconut cream
- ½ Madagascar vanilla pod, sliced in half lengthwise

For frosting
- 1 cup of cacao butter
- 1 cup of coconut cream
- 2 spoons of raw honey
- ¼ cup of coconut butter

- ½ cup of fresh or frozen raspberries
- ½ spoon of red beet powder
- 1 cup of fresh raspberries for the cream and décor
- 1 spoon of coconut flakes for décor

Preparation

Place all dry ingredients for the batter in the food processor and pulse a few times. Add the remaining ingredients and mix well.

Pour the batter in a round baking dish with a 17 cm diameter (6.6 inches).

Bake in the preheated oven for 15 minutes at medium heat (176°C or 350°F) or until the toothpick inserted in the middle comes out clean.

Let it cool and repeat for the second layer of the cake. If you have a taller baking dish you could double the ingredients for the batter, bake in one go and then slice the layer in half.

Until the cake layers cool, prepare the vanilla cream and the frosting.

To make the vanilla cream, mix all the ingredients for the cream in a bowl on a bain-marie (double boiler). With the peak of a knife scrape the inside of the vanilla pod inside the bowl. Add the vanilla pod as well and let them all slowly cook together.

Be careful that the bowl in which you are cooking the cream does not touch the boiling water with its bottom. Whisk constantly and keep heat at low. The cream needs to cook for about 25-30 minutes on bain-marie. Once you see it thickens, remove the vanilla pod, and let the cream cool.

Once cooled enough that it does not burn, pour the cream over the first layer. If you have extra cream left, eat it later with fresh fruit or freeze.

Add the raspberries on top, one by one, close to each other until there is no empty space left. I like to set them in two different positions near each other-one up and the other upside down. This way there is no empty space at all, and the cake is rich in fruit.

Place the second layer over the cream and let it set in the fridge for at least two hours.

To make the frosting, place the cacao butter, coconut butter and honey in a glass dish for bain-marie. Make sure the bowl in which you are preparing the frosting does not reach the boiling water underneath. Let them slowly melt while whisking.

Blend the raspberries in a blender or food processor. Pour the blended liquid through a sieve and remove the seeds. Keep just the pulp, seed-free. When the frosting ingredients are all melted and combined add the raspberry pulp and whisk well.

Let the frosting cool until it is thick enough to pour over the cake. With an offset spatula, spread a thin layer of it on the top and sides of the cake.

Decorate with raspberries on top and sprinkle the coconut flakes. Then chill until set, about 15 minutes.

Note: This cake is more delicious the following day.

Carrot and walnut cake

Ingredients

The ingredients below are for one single layer of the cake. Double for the two-layer cake or bake the batter one by one if you only have one small baking dish.

- 1 cup of almond flour
- ¼ cup of coconut flour
- ½ teaspoon of aluminum-free baking soda
- ¼ cup of raw honey
- 2 eggs
- ¼ cup of melted ghee
- ½ cup of finely grated carrot

- ¼ cup of almond milk
- ½ teaspoon of cinnamon powder
- ¼ teaspoon of nutmeg powder
- ¼ teaspoon of clove powder
- ¼ cup of ground walnuts
- ¼ cup of sugar-free raisins

For the cream

- 1 cup of coconut cream
- 1 spoon of raw honey
- ½ cup of ground walnuts

- ¼ cup of sugar-free raisins
- 1 teaspoon of gelatin
- 1 spoon of warm water

For frosting

- 1 cup of cacao butter
- 1 cup of coconut cream
- 2 spoons of raw honey

- ½ cup of coconut butter
- 1 cup of ground walnut

Preparation

Except for the walnuts and the raisins, place all the dry ingredients in the food processor and pulse a few times. Add the wet ingredients and make the batter.

Incorporate the walnuts and the raisins in the batter with a spoon.

Pour the batter in a round baking dish with a diameter of 17 cm (6.60 inches) and bake in the preheated oven, at medium heat (176°C or 350°F), for about 30 minutes or until the toothpick inserted in the middle comes out dry.

Let it cool and repeat for the second layer of the cake. If you have a taller baking dish you could double the ingredients for the batter, bake in one go and then slice the layer in half.

Until the cake layers cool, prepare the cream and the frosting.

Except for gelatin, place all ingredients for the cream in a bowl and mix well with a whisk.

Let the gelatin bloom in the spoon of warm water and mix until it completely dissolves. Once fully dissolved incorporate in the cream with a whisk. Let the cream thicken-this will take a little time. When it reaches the consistency of sour cream you can pour over the first layer. Build the cake by placing the second layer on top of the cream.

Let it set in the fridge for two hours.

Meanwhile, prepare the frosting.

To make the frosting, place the butters in a glass dish for bain-marie. Make sure the bowl in which you are preparing the frosting does not reach the boiling water underneath. Let them slowly melt while whisking.

Melt the butters first and then add the remaining ingredients for the frosting while whisking constantly.

Let the glazing cool at room temperature or in the fridge for a few minutes until it thickens enough to be able to pour it over the cake.

Be very careful, if you leave the glazing in the fridge too long, it will start hardening on the margins. From the moment it thickens to the moment is completely hard there is a very short time window to spread it all over the cake, so you need to move fast. After this it becomes too hard and needs remelting.

Once you frosted the cake, sprinkle the ground walnuts all over and "dress it up".

Note: This cake is more delicious if it chills in the fridge for a few hours.

Artisan peach tart

Ingredients

- 1 cup of almond flour
- 1 spoon and a half of coconut flour
- 1 spoon of raw honey
- ¼ cup of melted ghee
- 1 egg
- 2-3 peaches peeled off and sliced

Preparation

Except for peaches, place the ingredients in the food processor and mix to make the dough. When it gets at the right consistency, the dough tends to turn into a ball while spinning.

Wrap it in a piece of baking paper in the fridge for 10 minutes.

Meanwhile peel and slice the peaches.

Remove the dough from the fridge, stretch between two sheets of parchment paper to a thickness of about 0.5 cm (0.20 inches).

Leaving around 7 cm (2.7 inches) free space from the margins, place the peach slices in a circle shape one near the other until all the space is full. Fold up the sides of the pastry and pinch together any gaps. Do not worry about aspect-you can easily fix any cracks by pinching the dough together and besides, it does not need to look perfect. This is the beauty of an artisan tart.

Let it bake in the preheated oven, at medium heat (176°C or 350°F), for about 15 minutes. Pour the half spoon of honey on top and let it bake for another 5 minutes.

Let it cool before slicing and serve.

Almond crumble with apples and raspberries

Ingredients

- 2 cups of ground almonds
- 1 cup of fresh raspberries
- 2 apples, diced
- 1 spoon of raw honey plus another teaspoon and a half
- ¼ teaspoon of cinnamon powder
- ¼ teaspoon of nutmeg powder

Preparation

Heat up the apple with one spoon of honey, with the cinnamon and nutmeg and cook in a pan, at low heat, for 5 minutes, until they begin to caramelize.

Then mix the almonds with the raspberries. Pour the remaining honey on top and bake in the oven at medium heat (176°C or 350°F), for 15 minutes.

Serve after cooling.

I baked this in ramekins of 10 cm diameter and 5 cm height (4x2 inches).

Poached pear tart

Ingredients

For the poached pears

- 2 pears, cut into half, lengthwise
- 800 ml of water
- 2 spoons of raw honey

For the batter

- 1 cup and a half of almond flour
- 2 spoons of coconut flour
- 1 spoon of raw honey
- ¼ cup of ghee
- 2 eggs

For the cream

- 4 spoons of coconut flour
- 2 spoons of raw honey

- ½ a Bourbon de Madagascar vanilla pod (I chose this for the amazing flavor, but you can use any other type of vanilla)
- 1 cup of crushed raspberry

- 1 egg
- ¼ teaspoon of vanilla essence
- ½ cup of melted ghee
- ¼ teaspoon of vanilla powder
- ¼ teaspoon of aluminum free baking soda

For decor

- 4 spoons of almond flakes

Preparation

Poach the pears an evening before baking the tarts. It will allow the flavors to combine, and the pears will receive a stronger color.

To poach the pears, prepare a pot with 800 ml of water to boil. Cut the vanilla pod into two, scrape the content with the peak of a knife and place it with the pod in the boiling water. Crush the raspberry with your fingers and add in the pot with the honey.

When the water is boiling, turn the heat on low and add the pears. Let them boil slowly until they soften, around 15-25 minutes, depending on how ripe they are. Remove the pot and let it cool. It would be best if you could let it chill in the fridge until the next day.

Place the ingredients for the dough in the food processor and mix until the dough is dense and holding together like a ball.

Let it chill in the fridge for 10 minutes and then separate it in 4 equal parts. Mold each one in 4 different ramekins prepared for baking and greased with a little ghee and set aside.

Add all the dry ingredients for the cream in a bowl and whisk. Add all the remaining ingredients for the cream and whisk some more.

Pour the cream over the molded dough.

Place one piece of pear in each ramekin, pushing it down slowly until the margins fully submerse in the cream.

Sprinkle a spoon of almond flakes over the cream and near the pears in all ramekins.

Bake in the preheated oven for 25 minutes, at low heat (65°C or 150°F).

Let them cool and serve.

Sticky toffee pudding

Ingredients

For the batter

- 1 cup and a half of almond flour
- ½ cup of coconut flour
- ½ teaspoon of aluminum-free baking soda
- 3 eggs
- ¼ cup of melted ghee
- ½ cup of almond milk
- ½ cup of dates, soaked in warm water for 30 minutes (10-12 pieces)
- 3 apples, peeled and grated

For the caramel sauce

- ½ cup of ghee
- 1 cup of honey
- 2 cups of coconut cream

Preparation

Place all the dry ingredients for the batter in the food processor and pulse a few times. Add the eggs, ghee, milk, and dates and mix until you get a fine batter.

Incorporate the grated apples with a spoon.

Pour the batter in a square baking dish, prepared with baking paper, preferably a square of 24 cm (9.5 inches) each side.

Bake at medium heat (176°C or 350°F) for 30 minutes.

Meanwhile make the caramel sauce. Pour all ingredients for the sauce in a pan and cook at low heat until it thickens to a consistency of a pancake batter.

Remove the dish from the oven after the 30 minutes and make some holes in the cake with a spoon. Pour the sauce over. Some will fill in the holes and the rest will partially glaze the cake.

Bake for another 10 minutes, at low heat (65°C or 150°F).

Let it cool completely and then cut and serve.

Just a note that this cake is very rich in honey and nutrients and should be consumed in small portions.